MW00610403

DEVELOPING CONDOMINIUMS

Successful Strategies

Urban Land Institute

Copyright ©2006 by ULI–the Urban Land Institute

All rights reserved. No part of this book may be reproduced in any form or by any means, electronic or mechanical, including photocopying and recording, or by any information storage and retrieval system, without written permission of the publisher.

ULI–the Urban Land Institute
1025 Thomas Jefferson Street, N.W.
Suite 500 West
Washington, D.C. 20007-5201

ULI–the Urban Land Institute is a nonprofit education and research institute that is supported by its members. Its mission is to provide responsible leadership in the use of land in order to enhance the total environment.

ULI sponsors education programs and forums to encourage an open international exchange of ideas and sharing of experiences; initiates research that anticipates emerging land use trends and issues and proposes creative solutions based on that research; provides advisory services; and publishes a wide variety of materials to disseminate information on land use and development. Established in 1936, the Institute today has more than 30,000 members in over 80 countries, representing the entire spectrum of the land use and development disciplines. The Institute is recognized throughout the world as one of America's most respected and widely quoted sources of objective information on urban planning, growth, and development.

Library of Congress Cataloging-in-Publication Data
Bach, Alexa.
Developing condominiums : successful strategies / Alexa Bach.
   p. cm.
ISBN-13: 978-0-87420-963-1
1. Condominiums—Conversion—Case studies.   I. Title.
HD7287.66.B33 2006
333.33'8—dc22   2006017550

10 9 8 7 6 5 4 3 2 1
Printed in China.

Design and Composition
Marc Alain Meadows, Meadows Design Office Incorporated
Washington, D.C. www.mdomedia.com

Frontis Images
Opening page, the Terraces at EmeryStation, Emeryville, California (Heller Manus Architects); *title page spread,* Kensington Park, Richfield, Minnesota (Sam Newberg); *Acknowledgments page,* the Palmolive Building, Chicago, Illinois (Draper and Kramer); *Contents page,* Missouri Street Residences, San Francisco, California (John Sutton Photography).

Project Staff

Rachelle L. Levitt
Executive Vice President, Information Group
Publisher

Dean Schwanke
Senior Vice President, Publications and Awards

Adrienne Schmitz
Director, Residential Community Development

Alexa Bach
Scholar in Residence
Project Director

Nancy H. Stewart
Director, Book Program

Lori Hatcher
Director, Publications Marketing

James A. Mulligan
Managing Editor

Laura Glassman
Publications Professionals LLC
Manuscript Editor

Betsy VanBuskirk
Art Director

Craig Chapman
Director, Publishing Operations

Editors

Alexa Bach
Urban Land Institute
Washington, D.C.

Adrienne Schmitz
Urban Land Institute
Washington, D.C.

Introduction Author

Alexa Bach
Urban Land Institute
Washington, D.C.

**Contributing Authors
to the Introduction**

George Kelly
Urban Land Institute
Washington, D.C.

Brad Berton
Freelance Writer
Portland, Oregon

Case Studies Authors

The Bakery, 1400 on 5th
B. Kriesler
ImPrint, LLC
Manassas, Virginia

807 Eighteenth, Watermarke
Alexa Bach
Urban Land Institute
Washington, D.C.

Kensington Park
Sam Newberg
Joe Urban, Inc.
Minneapolis, Minnesota

Palmolive
Deborah Myerson
Deborah Myerson LLC
Bloomington, Indiana

Promenade Lofts
Stuart Steers
Freelance Writer
Denver, Colorado

The Stellina
Clair Enlow
Freelance Writer
Seattle, Washington

The Terraces at EmeryStation
Kenny Caldwell
Caldwell Communications
Oakland, California

Zocalo
Anne Frej
Urban Land Institute
Washington, D.C.

Acknowledgments

We are indebted to a host of people for their help, advice, and support in preparing these pages. First and foremost, thanks go to the many developers, architects, and planners who added immeasurably to this publication by working with the case study authors and by providing data, written materials, illustrations, and photographs. In addition, we greatly appreciate the dedication and skill of the case study authors who compiled this information into meaningful stories.

We thank Bob Diamond, Steve Etminani, David Lichterman, and David Mayhood for critiquing the introduction to the book. Much appreciation goes to Laura Glassman for editing the text to make the presentation clear and useful to readers. And a very special thank you goes to Marc Meadows of Meadows Design Office for his beautiful design work.

Finally, we would like to thank a number of Urban Land Institute staff members for the skill and dedication they contributed to the manuscript development and book publication processes: Rachelle Levitt, Gayle Berens, and Dean Schwanke for their guidance; Nancy Stewart and Jim Mulligan for managing the editing process; Betsy VanBuskirk for her management of the design and layout process; Craig Chapman for coordinating the publication process; and Lori Hatcher for ensuring that *Developing Condominiums* reaches a wide audience.

Alexa Bach
Adrienne Schmitz
Editors

CONTENTS

Introduction 2

Case Studies 39

DEVELOPING CONDOMINIUMS
Successful Strategies

INTRODUCTION

The rising tide of home prices, the increase in residential investment, and the number of sales since the early 1990s mark the longest and strongest housing boom in U.S. history. This unprecedented growth created sizzling housing markets in the fast-growing areas of Arizona; Florida; Hawaii; Washington, D.C.; Las Vegas; and southern California. While the national median home price grew approximately 50 percent from 1992 through 2005, home prices more than doubled in areas such as Boston, Miami, San Francisco, and Washington, D.C.[1]

The record-breaking escalation of home prices began to squeeze first-time and low- and middle-income buyers out of the market or force them to move farther out to suburban fringe areas. Since 2001, the number of metropolitan areas where the median home price exceeded four times the median income has grown from ten to 33. Outside those areas, however, real estate prices are more in line with household incomes. The Joint Center for Housing Studies at Harvard University studied 110 communities other than the hottest markets and reported that more than 75 percent had sustainable price-to-income ratios (less than 1:4). The Joint Center found that the number of metropolitan areas where more than half of all households live at least ten miles outside of central business areas tripled between 1970 and 2000, reflecting affordability-driven homebuying decisions. In six metropolitan areas, more than 20 percent of households lived at least 30 miles from the central business district.

Amid the euphoria of single-family home sales is the record-breaking condominium market. As of February 2006, the median sales price of a condominium ($214,000) topped that of a single-family home ($209,000).[2] According to Harvard University's Joint Center, condominium construction starts jumped from 71,000 in 2003 to 121,000 in 2004, a 70 percent increase. The center found little evidence in rental data to suggest that this increase was investor driven, instead explaining the increase as satisfying growth in owner demand.

Intrigued by condominium lifestyle, and, in some cases, affordability, buyers have driven condominium development into urban centers, suburban communities, and resort areas across the country. Condominiums became popular in the 1970s, when interest rates and housing costs were high. The market quickly grew, enabling those who could not afford or who did not want the responsibility of a single-family home to become homeowners. Today's market is driven more by lifestyle choice than by affordability. The large number of aging baby boomers, the resistance to sprawl, the movement back to the city, and the development of mixed-use communities all dovetail into the increasing popularity of condominiums.

The recent strength of the condominium market has convinced strongly branded companies, such as Post Properties,
an established rental apartment community developer, and
D.R. Horton, a large, national homebuilder, to expand their
product lines to include condominiums. Post announced the
creation of a new subsidiary (called Post Services Inc.) early in
2005 to build and convert condominiums in key markets across
the country. D.R. Horton built only single-family detached
homes until 1996, but condominiums and townhouses now
make up more than 17 percent of the company's business.

Just how big is the condominium market? According to
the U.S. Census Bureau's annual housing survey, more than 1
million condominiums were sold in 2004—about one for
every seven single-family homes sold. In many cases, homebuyers are choosing condominiums not because they are
cheaper, but because purchasers prefer the closer-in location,
low-maintenance lifestyle, urban amenities, investment potential, and option for use as a vacation home or housing for
college students.

How secure is the condominium market? Will it endure the
ups and downs of the economy? Housing industry pundits have
suggested every answer from a steady appreciation in value,
to a "soft" landing, to a dramatic burst of the condominium

**Intrigued by the lifestyle, buyers
have driven condominium
development into urban centers,
suburban communities, and
resort areas across the country.**
John Sutton Photography

In land-scarce Singapore, this five-story, 176-unit condominium complex called Glentrees provides residents with a lush central garden and pool. Studio Steed Pte., Ltd.

market bubble. The last response was largely fueled by the popularity of condominiums with investors and speculators, a demand that typically dries up as mortgage rates rise. Even with rising interest rates, many experts believe that aging baby boomers will continue to support condominium demand.

The word *condominium* describes not the physical characteristics of the property, but rather the legal ownership arrangement. The buyer takes ownership of a unit, typically an apartment in a multiunit building, but it could also be a housing unit in a cluster of rowhouses or even detached houses. Condominium ownership also exists in office, retail, and industrial property, but commercial property types are not included in this book. Typically, the condominium buyer individually owns everything from the unit's walls inward (although

A creative ownership structure helped finance the multiuse Time Warner Center in New York City. Instead of one landlord with multiple leases, a condominium regime was created in which each member now owns the fee interest in its condominium unit.
Uwe Ditz Photography

the unit boundaries can vary from project to project). The owners also jointly own the building structure and common areas—such as the land, lobby, hallways, swimming pool, and parking lot. Maintenance of the common areas becomes the responsibility of a condominium association. Most states require that a developer file a declaration of condominium (sometimes known as the master deed), which outlines the rights and obligations of each party, including those of the developer, the owners, and the condominium unit owners association (UOA). Unit owners automatically become members of the UOA and must pay a condominium fee, usually payable monthly, that is used for upkeep of the common areas and other amenities and services. Reserves for repairs and refurbishing are also part of the condominium fee.

Cooperative housing, also known as a co-op, is another type of ownership. It was first created in New York City in the late 1800s. Today, more than 1.5 million households live in homes owned and operated through a cooperative association. Co-ops include townhouses, garden apartments, mid- and high-rise apartments, and single-family houses. Unlike condominium ownership, in which owners actually own their designated unit, a co-op is owned by a corporation and each owner obtains a proportional share in the corporation plus exclusive use of a particular unit. Shares can be bought and sold at will, but ownership transfers usually require approval from the co-op board. Co-op owners also pay a monthly fee. In addition to a monthly contribution for management, maintenance, insurance, property taxes, utilities, and contributions to reserve funds, shareholders pay their proportionate share of an underlying mortgage, if one exists.

Whereas condominium buyers can pay off or refinance their mortgages, the blanket co-op mortgage is secured by all units, requiring co-op share owners to make payments as long as the blanket mortgage is outstanding. Co-op unit owners can get individual share loans secured by their membership or stock interest and by their proprietary lenders. A housing cooperative typically elects a board of directors. Although cooperative units are generally considered personal property, not real estate, Virginia, Pennsylvania, and the Model Real Estate Cooperative Act treat cooperative units as realty and provide for transfer by deed.

The Condominium Product

Widespread demand for condominiums has encouraged new condominium construction across the country. From the urban convenience of high-rise towers to the walkable, suburban neighborhoods created by garden-style communities, condominium projects are now found in small towns and large cities alike. As a whole, condominium buyers are primarily attracted by the lifestyle. Condominiums offer buyers the opportunity to own their own residence without pushing a mower around the lawn or to swim in a pool that they never have to clean. This maintenance-free lifestyle is attractive to a broad spectrum of demographic groups. Now that their children are gone, many empty nesters are looking to downsize and enjoy urban living. Young professionals typically are looking for not only affordability, but also lifestyle, such as short commutes and trendy amenities or fashionable areas. They are often buying and renovating older condominiums to secure an ideal location. Suburban garden-style condominiums provide expansive amenities for small families.

In addition to new construction, condominium development includes renovating existing buildings. Such "rehabs" can include apartment conversions, in which an existing apartment building or complex is upgraded to be sold to owners, and adaptive use of buildings that began life as nonresidential buildings. Reusing existing buildings is an extremely popular option in urban areas with limited land available for new construction, as well as a useful strategy for revitalizing blighted neighborhoods.

Apartment Conversions

Today's condominium demand is being met, in large part, by the conversion of rental apartments instead of new construction. Setting a record, almost 9,000 condominiums were sold

Lofts

Trendy residential lofts popped up in the late 20th century in cities like Boston, Chicago, and New York. Living quarters were carved from big-city industrial and commercial spaces with a refined but funky character. The original loft residences, however, did not carry such sophistication. New York City was home to the first lofts about 50 years ago, when artists transformed vacant warehouses into live/work space. It was not unusual for those early lofts not to have kitchens or private bathrooms. Struggling artists washed their dishes in buckets and accessed their units by freight elevators and stairwells.

Today's lofts maintain the architectural appeal with high ceilings (from 11 to 25 feet), abundant open space, few walls, huge windows, and exposed raw surfaces, but most have lost the affordable price tag. Some lofts still reuse character-filled old buildings, while others create the historical-chic ambience with new construction. The inherently industrial nature now mingles with granite countertops, stainless steel appliances, state-of-the-art lighting, rooftop pools, courtyards, and doormen.

Once an indicator of trendy districts in our nation's largest cities, lofts are now providing urban living in cities and suburbs across the country. Loft residences sell for anywhere from hundreds of thousands to several million dollars. The lifestyle is most appealing to single professionals and dual-income couples without children.

in San Diego County in 2005, 5,000 of which were apartment conversions. This figure accounted for almost half of the conversion homes sold in southern California. Several factors have driven this trend, including an increasing demand for home ownership, low interest rates, changing social and demographic trends, lack of developable land in desirable locations, increased construction costs for new developments, and the relatively low profitability of owning and operating rental property.

The developer typically upgrades the property's exterior, common areas, and unit amenities. Granite countertops, deluxe kitchen appliances, and wood floors are often added to individual units, depending on the competition and the market. Some developers build the cost of the upgrades into the sales price of the condominium units, while others provide buyers

The Jefferson at Penn Quarter, covering almost an entire city block in downtown Washington, D.C., rehabilitated the original 1855 facade and restored the historical Civil War headquarters of Clara Barton. Left, photographer unknown; above, S. Hinds

Condominium Hotels

Condominium hotels, first popular in the United States during the 1970s and 1980s, have recently resurfaced in high-traffic tourist destinations and urban locations. One of the hottest trends among luxury resorts is to incorporate some kind of ownership program, either converting existing hotel rooms into condominium units or building a condominium hotel from the ground up. The term condominium hotel refers both to hotels with attached condominium units that share amenities and to hotels that sell individual rooms in condominium ownership. Buyers enjoy the luxury of hotel amenities and typically have the opportunity to rent their units as hotel rooms when they are not using them. This advantage can offset the condominium's operating expenses and might contribute to the mortgage payment. Some of the branded condominium hotel operators that offer buyers sophisticated marketing programs, centralized reservation systems, and management expertise include Intrawest, Marriott, Ritz-Carlton, and Starwood. Local and international buyers who want second or vacation homes, corporations buying units for executive suites, and sports figures who want a road-game residence typically purchase condominium hotel units. The condominium owner pays most unit expenses as well as some projectwide expenses, such as grounds maintenance, repairs, supplies, and management fees. The owner's agreement specifies the exact responsibilities of the developer and the owner.

Developers benefit from condominium hotels in several ways. The profit margin depends on the local market, but a 100 percent markup over development costs is standard. The developer also receives revenue from room rentals, food and beverage services, and other hotel amenities. Room revenue is usually split with the condominium unit owner and to a smaller degree with a third-party management company (if hired). According to Art Buser, managing director for Jones Lang LaSalle Hotels, the most common pitfall during condominium hotel development is adding too many amenities and overpricing the units for the market. He suggests interviewing residential brokers to understand what buyers want in terms of storage space, features, and length-of-stay rights.

Historic preservation is often an intricate process. In this case (facing page), the facades of four buildings were suspended in midair while the project was built below, behind, and above. A. Caballero

Midway through construction of Watermarke (right), a 535-unit luxury multifamily community in Irvine, California, the Sares·Regis Group recognized that the market was demanding for-sale product and decided to sell the units as condominium homes. Alexa Bach

the choice to purchase higher-quality finishes and features as separately priced options or option packages. Utilities may need to be reconfigured as well. If the building operated under a single heating and cooling system, that system is frequently converted to individual heating, ventilating, and air conditioning (HVAC) units and electric meters so that owners are responsible for their own utility costs. Water meters can also be installed for individual units.

The conversion process involves changing a multifamily property from single ownership with renters to condominium ownership with owner/occupants. This transfer adds an additional layer of complexity to the condominium development process. In addition to marketing to new buyers, complying with condominium laws, mitigating liability, and creating a UOA, converters must handle existing tenants. The choice with respect to tenants is whether or not to evict. The landlord can evict a rental tenant (except senior citizens and persons with disabilities) under certain conditions that vary from state to state. The eviction plan might require condominium presales or allow the tenant to complete the lease after the conversion is complete. The details of a plan without eviction are highly dependent on the locality. This approach generally applies to

buildings with rent-stabilized and rent-controlled tenants who do not desire to purchase their units. In this case, developers can sell only a limited percentage of those apartments as condominium units, and the tenants are allowed to renew their leases after the conversion is complete.

To streamline the conversion process, many developers are mapping and titling their projects as condominium communities upfront. This strategy requires inclusion of a clause in each rental agreement stating that the project is, in fact, owned as a condominium community and can be sold as individual condominiums. In most markets, lenders, attorneys, marketing firms, and property managers with specialized conversion experience can assist in this complex process.

The seemingly unstoppable acceleration of condominium conversions has many experts concerned about the risks of oversupply. When mortgage rates increase, condominium conversions may become even riskier. Slowing sales can result in an oversupply of condominiums and price reductions in some markets. Some converters contend that the affordability of conversions, in comparison to new construction, will be more attractive to homebuyers and help protect their investment.

Adaptive Use

Old buildings often outlive their original purpose. Adaptive use is a way to find new uses for these secondhand structures. Chic transformations draw tenants to downtowns and garner tremendous support from local government and community development corporations. Community encouragement can speed up the approval process and reduce dissent at public hearings, thus minimizing the long-term risk faced by urban condominium developers.

Before embarking on an adaptive use project, a team of architects, engineers, and environmental and planning consultants should investigate the site "as built." Historic structures should be inventoried. A preservation architect can propose an approach for reuse that will conform to the Secretary of the Interior's guidelines for the preservation and reuse of historic buildings and can determine whether the project is eligible for historic preservation tax credits.[3]

Older buildings may not meet the latest regulatory codes for the site. Wider hallways or parking spaces might be required by the Americans with Disabilities Act (ADA), and the fire code could require updating electrical systems and retrofitting sprinklers or fire walls. Title III of the ADA, which covers places of public accommodation and commercial facilities, applies to the areas within a condominium building or community that are not intended for the exclusive use of residents and their guests. Such facilities include all retail and commercial space, encompassing the condominium real estate office and associated model units, parking, entrances, access routes, and restrooms.[4] In addition to safety and accessibility, the mechanical and structural systems of the building need examination. The foundation needs to support the weight of the new design and usage, and the roof might need to be reinforced to carry new mechanical systems. An energy audit will determine whether additional venting or insulation is needed.

An environmental site assessment tests for contamination both within the building and on the site. Mold, lead-based paint, asbestos, petroleum distillates, and other contaminants require remediation that can increase cost and delay project construction. Developed by the U.S. Green Building Council, the Leadership in Energy and Environmental Design–Existing Buildings (LEED-EB) green building rating system provides guidelines for minimizing the environmental impact of construction and renovations within existing buildings.

Entry-Level Lofts Come to Downtown Minneapolis

Stevens Square, a longstanding neighborhood located just south of downtown Minneapolis, is a densely populated area consisting mostly of 1920s-era brown-brick apartment buildings. A transitional neighborhood, it remains popular with young professionals who enjoy its urban feel and proximity to downtown. However, it predominantly offers rental housing, leaving few owner options after residents have outgrown their apartments.

Recognizing this drain on the community, the Stevens Square Community Organization dedicated neighborhood revitalization project funds from the city to develop a for-sale condominium project marketed first to longtime neighborhood renters, then to the general public. In addition, the developer, Brighton Development, sought subsidies to make the project affordable to people in a wide range of income brackets. The Lofts on Arts Avenue, completed in 2004, is the first major residential project constructed in the neighborhood in more than 20 years.

The project design draws on the traditional architectural elements of the neighborhood in scale and materials, while offering a contemporary form and aesthetic as well as urban densities on a site that had been partly vacant and partly occupied by a boarding house. The original brick supplier for the old apartment buildings developed a custom blend of brick for the project based on materials used in those other buildings. A zoning variance allowed the building to extend to the property line to reinforce the street edge. Large commercial aluminum storefront windows maximize light inside the units, and the interior spaces are arranged around kitchen/bathroom cores, resulting in fewer traditional rooms with doors and more flexible space.

All 36 units were sold before construction was completed, about one-third to people already renting in the neighborhood, at prices ranging from $70,000 to $275,000. The success of this project is credited with generating new interest in the area, and several other new housing projects are now under construction.

Reprinted with permission from *Urban Land*, May 2005, published by the Urban Land Institute.

Condominium Project Feasibility

The development of condominiums is fundamentally different from that of other types of multifamily housing. Those differences present developers with a new set of risks and opportunities.

Due diligence is required before making any decisions about developing or converting a condominium project. Prior to buying land or beginning development, the developer should acquire a thorough understanding of the environmental, legal, and financial components of the property and how those attributes will affect marketing and development. These analyses focus on four elements: the market, the site, applicable regulations, and financial feasibility.

Market Analysis

Understanding the market is fundamental to a development's financial success.[5] The market analysis is critical for establishing the development concept and can help the development team become familiar with a new product type or geographical area. Demographic and economic characteristics of area households define the target market. Classic principles of supply and demand tell the developer what amenities, unit features, and prices appeal to the target buyer and what opportunities exist in the marketplace. Developers working in locations with a wide choice of condominium communities use the market analysis to find amenities and services that set their projects apart from the competition. Market studies also enable developers to survey local or regional markets when contemplating geographic expansion, gathering information about available land, and determining feasible locations from the standpoint of costs and regulatory constraints. The most successful developers use market research and their intuition to foresee changes in the urban fabric before their competition.

The market analysis begins by identifying regional population and household trends, recent and anticipated changes in the economic base, and employment patterns of the regional setting where the proposed development will occur. The analysts then narrow the focus to the county or city for more specific information, such as housing needs, regulatory issues, and transportation patterns. Target market areas are the locations where the majority of demand for the proposed condominium project exists. Four demographic factors are used to analyze the target areas: employment growth, population projections, household demand, and average income. Analysts then look at the current and projected housing stock in the competitive market area. This inventory should examine successful and not-so-successful projects and what makes

The Lofts on Arts Avenue (facing page) created a home-ownership opportunity for Minneapolis residents living in the transitional Stevens Square neighborhood. Brighton Development

The first phases of development at Zocalo (above), a condominium community in Santa Fe, New Mexico, included several two-floor unit types. These units proved less popular with the target market, so future phases will include more single-level units. Alan Stoker Photography

them so. Overall sales pace, absorption, average square footage, price per square foot, unit mix, standard features, amenities, and upgrade options are all studied.

Site Selection

The project's success hinges on the compatibility of the site with the development concept. Site selection involves balancing location with land cost, its suitability for development, and the developer's vision. The higher density and more cost-effective use of land suits condominiums for a wider range of locations than single-family housing. High-rise condominiums work well in downtown settings where land is usually too expensive to support single-family detached housing. Within and outside the urban core, mid- and low-rise condominiums can blend the transition between office and residential buildings in a mixed-use neighborhood. Developers should consider past city growth trends when picking a site. Easy access to the

Baum/Thornley Architects carefully designed 10th Street Lofts in San Francisco to meet today's market demands. Units are sized and configured to provide spacious living environments that sell at desirable prices. John Sutton Photography

Former home to a flagship retail store, the site for One Beacon Court (facing page), was acquired by purchasing retailer Alexander's common stock over a 20-year period. Jeff Goldberg/ESTO

property and to public transportation is an important asset. Additional land or rights-of-way might be necessary to redirect site access, especially if the site borders undesirable land uses. Condominium developments near employment, commercial, and recreational centers are generally easier to market than less convenient properties.

In many cases, developers have to conceive a project around a site they already own. These sites require significant vision and creativity to ensure success and may require builders to create their own demand. For example, the Sares·Regis Group (SRG) purchased two parcels of land in Irvine, California, in 2000—one for an apartment community and the second for an office complex. After holding the land for a few years, SRG noted a change in market conditions and decided to build a condominium community on the first site and to sell the second parcel because of the lack of demand for office space.

Regulatory Approvals

The regulatory and legal context for condominiums has evolved over the years as a result of efforts to reduce discrimination, unsafe conditions, and the negative effects of development on neighborhoods and the environment. Developers and builders now need to spend more time studying the development site and scrutinizing the relevant legislation governing condominium development to ensure the proposed project is feasible and to facilitate the approvals process.

The Fair Housing Act, the Americans with Disabilities Act (ADA) of 1990, various environmental laws, and applicable state and local laws are of prominent importance. The Fair Housing Act emphasizes an individual's right to decent housing as determined by the secretary of the U.S. Department of Housing and Urban Development. The secretary conducts studies of suspected discriminatory housing practices in specially selected communities throughout the United States. The results of those studies are published in report form, providing recommendations to other federal, state, and local public and private agencies, as well as Congress, for eliminating discriminatory housing practices. The ADA guarantees handicapped individuals access to 12 categories of public accommodation. In addition to offering ADA-approved units, a developer has to make the condominium models, parking, and sales offices accessible. If making the sales areas ADA compliant is too expensive for the developer, the act allows the sales agent to meet with the prospective buyer at any other mutually agreeable location that is accessible.

Environmental due diligence is extremely important when selecting a site. An assortment of cross-cutting federal envi-

Vornado Realty Trust, developer of One Beacon Court in New York City, overcame a pending zoning change and complete design overhaul after the foundations had been poured. Kevin Chu/KCJP

ronmental laws might apply to the site, ranging from specific legislation regarding endangered species, historic preservation, and wetlands preservation, to more general laws such as the National Environmental Policy Act and the Clean Water Act. The Comprehensive Environmental Response, Compensation, and Liability Act and Amendments, also called the Superfund Law, identifies and assesses liability for hazardous waste sites. The 1986 amendments provide that landowners with no prior knowledge of contamination are not held liable for the pollution if they can prove that environmental due diligence was part of the development process. Additionally, developers working with a contaminated site might be eligible for federal funding through the Brownfield Economic Redevelopment Initiative of the U.S. Environmental Protection Agency. During condominium redevelopment, developers should watch out for asbestos, lead, pesticides, chlorofluorocarbons, radon, and underground storage tanks. Improperly maintained HVAC systems can be breeding grounds for illness-causing microorganisms. Leaking roofs or windows can cause mold or mildew.

Before pursuing a project, the development team should confirm that zoning and restrictive covenants allow for the proposed condominium development. Sites governed by flexible, floating, and performance zones may allow more creativity within the site plan. Other pertinent state and local laws include building and fire codes, impact and development fees, and regulations governing condominium conversions.

Financing

By 2006, as lenders for condominium construction and conversion have become more cautious amid concerns about oversupplies of condominium units in some markets, developers have been finding it necessary to fill the gap between on-hand cash and acquisition or construction debt with additional mezzanine-type capital or investor equity.

Through much of 2005, proven developers and converters were typically able to secure as much as 80 or even 85 percent of a venture's expected overall acquisition, improvement, construction, and sales costs from primary lenders. A typical capital structure would also include sponsor equity and mezzanine debt, each amounting to 5 to 10 percent of a project's cost.

But today, the commercial banks and other lenders providing the primary debt are in most cases willing to fund at only 75 to 80 percent loan-to-cost, leaving the sponsor to secure higher-cost capital to fill the funding gap. Sponsors tend to shoot for at least 90 percent overall leverage through primary and mezzanine debt, and in many cases they can combine primary and secondary sources to secure as much as 95 percent of expected costs. Under the lower loan-to-cost ratios primary lenders are providing today, however, the additional costs of the secondary financing essentially represent a relinquishing of venture profits the developer or converter could have pocketed under the primary leverage levels available previously.

Mezzanine debt remains by far the capital-stack gap-filler of choice, especially for condominium converters and for some new project developers—although sponsors might look to cover varying portions of the gap with even higher-cost straight and preferred equity.

The primary financing is usually variable-rate debt, in many cases floating at somewhere between 300 and 400 basis points over the 30-day or 90-day LIBOR rate. Some banks might instead quote a spread over their prime rates, with others offering borrowers a choice. This debt is first-priority and secured by the real estate, and in most cases it requires personal recourse commitments from the individual borrowers. Typical term lengths are 18 to 36 months.

Local, regional, national, and global commercial banks tend to be the main sources of primary acquisition/conversion and construction debt, although various specialty finance operations and even pension funds of construction trades might pursue such financings. The sponsors pay interest only on the outstanding balance and are required to maintain a reserve account to cover interest payments.

Conversions are generally considered less risky than from-scratch new developments because market conditions are less likely to deteriorate during the quicker unit renovations and sales. Hence, available construction loan-to-cost ratios tend to be a bit lower than conversion comparables within a given marketplace (although rate spreads are usually the same).

With conversions, banks typically fund enough initially to cover the bulk of the property purchase price and release additional funds for unit and common area improvements when specified levels of unit presales are achieved. Most of the unit sales proceeds are pledged to repay principal. Primary lenders have typically required that the sponsor negotiate presales of 15 to 30 percent of the units before opening the first escrow. Some cities might require converters to assist with tenant relocation costs.

With new condominium construction ventures, primary lenders initially release funds covering the site acquisition as well as any predevelopment site work and the costs of presales efforts. Hard construction funds are released to fund the vertical construction, with lenders in some markets still requiring some degree of presales.

Likewise, the leverage level and pricing of the primary debt for both conversions and construction varies by numerous factors, including market conditions and a sponsor's track record and equity sources. With conversions, such factors might also include the extent of the planned improvements and even the price being paid for the rental community. Generally speaking, the primary interest rate rises commensurately with the loan-to-cost leverage level.

Those same factors help determine the pricing of the mezzanine component, which is secured by interests in the property's ownership entity, rather than by deeds of trust recorded against the real estate. With condominium conversions and developments today, mezzanine lenders typically expect a fixed-rate yield of 15 to 20 percent—again depending on various factors and especially the sponsor's track record.

Mezzanine lenders have become more reluctant to invest in from-scratch developments, instead remaining active with conversions. Developers of small condominium projects tend to seek out other individual investors to fill the gap, whereas pension funds and multi-investor opportunity funds invest in larger projects by proven players (which might convince primary lenders to boost loan-to-cost ratios). Although more costly than mezzanine capital, straight and preferred equity are also more patient and flexible when projects take longer than expected.

The Stellina, an affordable condominium community in downtown Seattle, was financed by a \$3.6 million loan from Homestreet Bank and additional support from LISC (Local Initiative Support Corporation), a national nonprofit community development financing corporation.
Clair Enlow

Mezzanine components typically represent 10 to 15 percent of a conversion venture's capital stack, but even 20 percent is not unheard of now that primary lenders have become more cautious with leverage. Under strong sales activity, sponsors might look to refinance mezzanine debt with additional lower-cost primary debt secured by the remaining unit inventory.

A select number of capital sources might provide both primary and mezzanine debt for a condominium conversion, which eliminates duplicated origination fees and the need for an intercreditor agreement.

From-scratch developers might also be able to secure financing subsidies for constructing units reserved for sale to low- or moderate-income buyers. This type of development can reduce capital costs, but it may well entail paying construction crews under prevailing wages regulations. Some cities require an affordable element with any housing development, subsidized or otherwise.

Securing an agreeable financing scheme is essential to closing a first-rate condominium deal. Successful strategies for financing condominium development include the following:

» **Educate the lender.** Demonstrate that you understand your market. This strategy may include literally driving the lenders around the area and showing them comparable projects—especially those projects that show a premium will be paid for something equivalent to your product. The tour validates the appraisal process and unit pricing schematic. Superior quality and a niche product are often essential to obtain favorable underwriting. A unique product that can be differentiated from the competition is easier to sell to lenders.

Gap financing from a variety of sources helped make 24 condominium homes at Lofts on Arts Avenue in Minneapolis affordable to those at incomes ranging from 50 to 115 percent of area median income. Brighton Development

» **Designate the target buyers.** It is the developer's responsibility to identify the target buyers and demonstrate that they have the income potential and are willing to absorb the product. Demonstrate demand for your product by locating where your buyers currently live, their migration patterns, and their existing housing choices.

» **Demonstrate site control.** A document proving ownership of the site or showing the property is under contract is necessary for the lender's review.

» **Build a solid loan package.** The lender uses the loan package to determine a proposed project's viability. The package includes a pro forma, comparable property analysis, schematic drawings and renderings, entitlements, demographic analysis, and preliminary cost estimates. Photographs of comparable projects are very helpful in assisting the lender with understanding the project. Equity sources should be documented, as well as the experience and background of the entire management team. Environmental and geotechnical testing are also necessary in most cases.

» **Size loan values, returns, and interest rates appropriately.** The value of the loan will increase based on the perceived accuracy of the loan package. The lender will be more apt to provide the requested financing if convinced that the deal can be accomplished as it is underwritten and that the developer will be able to deliver the product on time and according to the agreed upon pro forma. An 80 percent construction loan, a 10 percent mezzanine loan, and 10 percent equity contribution are typical.

» **Develop a marketing program before meeting with lenders.** A well-constructed marketing program helps the lender envision the as-yet unbuilt project. A virtual tour, knockout sales office, and well-designed models enable both buyers and lenders to experience the project before breaking ground. Lenders may ask to interview the sales force or to see their resumes.

» **Select high-quality general contractors.** Lenders will strictly scrutinize the past performance of your general contractor and subcontractors. Ensure that you conduct your due diligence and verify the general contractor's track record and ability to complete the job on time and on budget.

» **Be upfront.** Practice full disclosure with the lender, regardless of risk. The lender does not want to be surprised by even small bumps in the road.

Project and Site Design

Success in the condominium business revolves around delivering what homebuyers want as quickly and as cheaply as possible. Standard factors considered during the project planning phase include site planning, parking, exterior architecture, interior mix and design, and project amenities. Thinking beyond the technical elements to create a sense of place for the target market is also important. The density or cost analysis will not matter if the desired buyers are not attracted to the project. For example, to target empty nesters or young professionals, the land planner or architect may allocate less square footage for residential units and more space for amenities and services. Nevertheless, move-down buyers generally want spacious units with generous storage and upgraded finishes comparable to what they left behind in their previous homes.

Site Planning

Consider what a prospective owner will see when driving up to the project, entering the sales office, and walking into each condominium home. How do the balconies look from the street, and what views do the windows offer? Noisy streets or neighbors might require an open space or tree-line buffer.

Well-designed site plans choose a density, parking layout, and emergency access route that respect the natural characteristics of the land and its surroundings. Low-rise condominium buildings, such as Zocalo in Santa Fe, New Mexico, use densities of less than 30 units per acre to blend with existing suburban communities, whereas urban high-rise condominiums, such as the Palmolive in Chicago, Illinois, apply densities three times greater to mingle with neighboring office buildings and hotels.

Developers planning a condominium project should consider market demands and public concerns as well as their own needs. Heightened sensitivity to community qualms can speed up the approvals process and reduce plan revisions. The site planning process includes three stages: concept planning, preliminary planning, and final planning. The concept plan is often created before the developer commits to a specific site. This stage allows the developer to try out alternative building configurations, site sizes, general amenities, locations for open space, and road placement. Base maps are prepared showing site boundaries and existing features. A regulatory analysis identifies all local, state, and federal requirements for plan submission and review. By the end of the first stage, the developer should have articulated the optimal development program—specifying the mini-

Many projects are catering to residents' post-9/11 security concerns with monitored entries and 24-hour concierges. Uwe Ditz Photography

Facing page: Working closely with the community, Baum/ Thornley Architects created 22 two-level condominium units in 11 four-story townhouses at Lofts at Arts Avenue, distinctive in style, yet carefully configured to blend seamlessly with the existing locale. John Sutton Photography

mum number of dwelling units, type of amenities, character of the project, and nonresidential uses on site.

The preliminary planning stage refines the concept plan and creates an illustrative site plan. The schematic is a working drawing that continues to change as the local government and the developer make commitments regarding the total number of units, building types, roadway configuration, and amount of open space. Topographic, boundary, and utility surveys anchor the illustrative plan to reality. Site-specific field investigations and the environmental impact assessment further distill the concept plan. At this point, the preliminary plan is submitted to the local planning commission for review. The planning staff members can distribute copies to appropriate

Shared driveways allow more space for a green street presence in urban areas.

John Sutton Photography

local, state, and federal agencies for review, then incorporate all comments into a report of findings. The iterative process continues into the final planning stage. Changes to the final plan are usually in response to changing the product type or unit mix to better respond to the market.

Parking

The land area designated for parking often amounts to more than that assigned to the condominium units themselves. Zoning usually determines the minimum number of spaces, but market studies help decide whether more spaces are necessary. Dimensions, arrangement, and location depend on the location of building entrances, aesthetic appeal, and cost. When designing the parking configuration, the development team should consider how the final design will affect the feel of the community. Can private parking areas increase the feeling of security and ownership? How can a several-story parking garage seamlessly blend with the condominium community? For example, the roof of a mostly underground parking garage can be carpeted with grass and turned into a parklike community amenity. Or, as in the case study on Watermarke in Irvine, California, the condominium buildings can entirely wrap around the parking facilities. Wrap-style parking makes the multilevel garage invisible from outside the community and allows residents to park only steps from their unit doors.

Exterior Architecture

Exterior product design should reflect market demands and site limitations. Chosen materials and architectural elements should indicate the target buyers' preferences. Higher prices demand a higher quality of materials. However, good design need not always cost more. The style of the condominium project should be compatible with local architectural trends, existing development, or both. Regional traditions and climate are important for defining this style. A shallow or flat roof may work well in warmer Floridian climates but would not be the best choice for the rain and snow of northern regions. Balconies work best when architecturally integrated into the building. The usability of a balcony depends on its size. Smaller areas cannot serve as living spaces, while very deep balconies might excessively shade the unit or the one below.

Interior Mix and Design

In general, for-sale housing requires higher-grade finishes and amenities than rental housing and, as a result, calls for higher-quality subcontractors than apartment development. Special attention should be given to cabinetry, countertops, lighting, and flooring. Square footage and floor plans, finishes, and amenities should all reflect the target market. Market research suggests the appropriate number and type of condominium units per project based on the vacancies and overall demand of the local area. If the target market is predominantly singles and young couples, the project will need more studio and one-bedroom units. The development team can determine the optimal number of baths; placement for windows, doors, cabinetry, and utility areas; and the need for extra options, such as sunrooms, dens, and lofts. If the project is targeting a certain niche market, such as single students or young professionals sharing a unit, a special floor plan may be necessary.

The primary objective for condominium unit design is to make the space feel larger than it is. Large windows, open floor plans, and high ceilings create the impression of more space. Placing the entrance to a room on a diagonal axis can make that area feel larger than if the door were centrally located on a wall. Creatively shaped condominium units offer more design opportunities than rectangular ones. Adequate storage areas in the kitchen and elsewhere are essential to make the condominium feel livable and larger. Most condominium projects will need in-unit laundry facilities and fully equipped kitchens (dishwashers, disposals, and built-in microwaves). Depending on the target market, baths might require large soaking tubs, separate showers, and double vanities.

Large, expansive windows and a diagonally placed entrance give a small unit an open, spacious feel. John Sutton Photography

A diverse array of skylights, windows, and light wells brightens the 18 live/work condominiums at Florida Street Lofts in San Francisco. John Sutton, Sharon Risendorph

Condominium homes are blended with retail, office, hotel, and cultural space at the Time Warner Center. Jazz at Lincoln Center, a performance venue (facing page), is located in the heart of the building, on floors six through ten. Jim D'Addio, Rafael Viñoly Architects

Condominium finishes should be chosen for style, durability, and ease of maintenance. Uniform window treatments should be standard in all units because they improve the look of the individual condominium home and increase the value of the overall project. Common custom features include fireplaces, individual security systems, and garages.

Building layouts should provide privacy regardless of the project's density. The design of fences, walls, balconies, and landscaping should ensure that residents cannot see directly into other homes. Minimizing the number of community entries provides greater traffic control and improved security. All walkways should be well lit and visible from several points.

Considering the risk of the chosen design is important. A very elaborate or large-scaled design may require phasing, which is not feasible under all financing strategies. Concrete might be the least-expensive building material, but it does not always create the most value for the density. Land values can significantly influence the configuration of a product. If a higher-density design is suitable for the program and site, it can save a considerable amount of money, depending on the price of land. Expensive lots require a design with more square footage (higher density) to ensure a profit.

Amenities

The market analysis is a good place to start for selecting the project's amenities. Include only amenities for which the target market is willing to pay. Play areas work well in projects targeting families with children, whereas wide trails used for walking, running, and biking can appeal to many buyers. These items are low cost. Higher-cost amenities like pools are also popular at most price levels, especially with attractive deck areas for sunning and socializing. Diving boards and deep ends, however, have disappeared from condominium projects because of liability issues. Indoor amenities, such as fitness centers and party rooms, are popular in northern climates and urban locations with limited land. Wired and wireless Internet capability are almost essential in most markets.

Trends

Today, designers of condominiums are spending most of their time appealing to young professionals and empty nesters moving back to the city in search of contemporary, loft-inspired spaces. "What is key," explains David Graham, principal of South Carolina–based Graham Group Architecture, "is that new projects are not isolated from the public realm. Rather than replicating traditional architectural language, we are interested in innovative architectural materials and expression,

The three- and four-bedroom layouts at Missouri Street Residences, each featuring a "great room" with a high ceiling and some with bonus family rooms and penthouse master suites, are designed to appeal to growing, multiple-generation families. John Sutton Photography

The use of natural wood windows, trim, beams, and trellises recalls the richness of turn-of-the-century timber warehouses (facing page), appealing to the next generation of loft dwellers.
John Sutton Photography

but within the city's traditional fabric." Some examples are mixing materials such as brick and cement plaster or using pitched metal roofs and metal mesh sunscreens to blend new projects into an existing context without overwhelming the historic character. Designers are producing what Michael Willis, founding principal of Michael Willis Architects, headquartered in San Francisco, calls variegated design, fluctuating in height, width, and materials to bridge the gap between the old and the new architecture and steering away from blocks of starkly repetitive design.

A small portion of urban product is designed with a children's component—usually a playground or a kids' club—for young professionals with families or empty nesters who are grandparents.

Across the board, condominiums now include higher-quality finishes than in the past, especially in the kitchens. Buyers are also choosing nine-foot-high ceilings, open kitchens, multiple large windows, and remote-controlled gas (instead of wood-burning) fireplaces. Cork, bamboo, and concrete floors are also popular, as are transparent panels that allow light to penetrate deeper into units. In some metropolitan areas, developers are choosing "liner units," which provide parking for condominium owners but hide the spaces from the street. In this case, parking is usually tucked behind a row of residential or retail buildings.

W. Harris "Bill" Smith, partner of Smithfield Properties, Chicago, had a bold vision for the 25-story Erie on the Park. "Our goal was to differentiate our product from everything else in the marketplace," says Smith. The parallelogram-shaped, steel-and-glass building sits northwest of the Loop in Chicago's River North neighborhood. Initially envisioned as a concrete structure, Erie on the Park was the city's first steel-

framed high-rise residential building in more than 50 years. Concrete had been the preferred choice for mid- and high-rise residential buildings because it more easily met floor-height and fire-safety requirements and was typically cheaper because the structural frame could also serve as the exterior facade. Erie's steel frame appealed to architect Lucien Lagrange because it allowed for longer column spans; smaller columns; more flexibility in the distribution of the mechanical, electrical, and plumbing (M/E/P) systems; and intriguing exterior design possibilities. The 37-foot span of the steel columns, as opposed to concrete construction, which has a 20-by-20-foot grid, allowed the design team to create 23 different unit configurations—a significant selling point. Smithfield used a compressed design schedule to get the building to market as quickly as possible. The three design stages—foundation, superstructure, and M/E/P systems/tenant buildout—were chronologically based on the permit acquisition process. Erie on the Park exceeded Smith's original bold vision. More than 60 percent of the 125 units were sold before ground breaking, during the first two weeks on the market, with the remainder soon after. Sales averaged a 10 percent premium over similar condominium projects in the area.

Marketing and Sales

Marketing is about results. The marketing team, which may be hired consultants or in-house professionals, constructs a solid merchandising, marketing, and pricing strategy to add value to the entire project; the team manages sales velocity and maximizes profits. For maximum results, the marketing team should be involved in the project from ground breaking until the last sale is closed so that it can help make important design and planning decisions.

Cristalla

Owners at Cristalla, a 197-residence condominium tower in downtown Seattle, have no-cost, 24-hour access to a new Honda Civic LX hybrid parked in their private garage. The developer, Cristalla LLC, partnered with Flexcar, the nation's largest car-sharing company, to create an exclusive program for Cristalla buyers. Residents reserve the shared car by using Flexcar's online reservation service or automated phone system, or by contacting the building's full-service concierge.

Steve Keating Photography

Many marketing and sales agencies focus solely on multifamily communities or condominiums. These agents are specially trained to understand the particular wants and needs of a condominium buyer; they will develop a targeted campaign specific to the property.

Developers should select a team whose members will see their responsibilities through to completion, who think proactively and expeditiously to find solutions, and who demonstrate up-to-date knowledge and skills in the industry and the willingness and creative ability to improve their services.

In general, the marketing and sales team is responsible for defining the target market, creating a strategy to reach potential buyers, and implementing the sales plan. The team should begin gathering market research before development begins. Analysts determine the market demand for a given project and develop a purchaser profile. From this profile, they recommend development strategies regarding building amenities, architectural design, community name and theme, pricing, and product types. Focus groups are often used to assess a product's market appeal. The marketing and sales team will also recommend, select, and coordinate use of necessary professionals, such as advertising agencies, public relations firms, interior and graphic designers, and landscape architects.

The initial analysis should include a marketing audit, which surveys the competitors' ability to market their properties. Competitors' materials and marketing campaigns are critiqued to determine the most effective way to market the condominium property. The marketing budget of other projects is estimated by requesting rates from the publications where they place their ads. This information is helpful in defining the project's marketing strategy, plan, and budget.

The marketing plan begins as soon as the construction loan is approved. The plan outlines what tasks will be accomplished, the associated cost for each task, and the quantifiable results expected. The developer should review the marketing plan to confirm that the plan is adequate, is appropriate, and operates at a rational cost. After the marketing and sales plan is approved, the team should review legal documents for accuracy and factual consistency.

Real-world application of the marketing plan includes running an advertising campaign, handling on-site hiring of marketing and sales staff, and managing events such as the ground breaking and the grand opening. Those members of the development team involved in condominium sales will supervise the creation of the sales and design center and select model units, office displays, and furnishings as necessary. The team manages any required presales and associated promotions, and

proactively and routinely adjusts pricing on the available condominium units. Prospective and confirmed buyers are tracked in a computer database and invited to all community events.

The plan's success is measured by the absorption rate, or the average number of new sales per week. A low absorption rate indicates that the sales plan needs reassessment. High absorption rates could indicate an excellent marketing effort, pent-up demand for the product, or that the sales prices were too low and should be adjusted. Careful, ongoing analysis of sales is important for the best performance.

The Markethouse Lofts in San Jose, California, boosted presales with a single-family home sale technique—a full-scale model condominium created in neighborhood retail space. The Markethouse's triangular site had very little street frontage, leaving it virtually invisible to passersby, unlike the high-traffic storefront. The street-level sales gallery gave first-time buyers a true sense of condominium living, allowing them to experience the life-sized, furnished model while the 53-unit infill project was under construction. The developer was able to showcase an assortment of finishes and details throughout the model and provided prospective buyers with a computer-generated tour of the project and models on DVD to take home. In the end, the off-site model mock-up sparked sales for the Markethouse Lofts, a cornerstone of a city revitalization effort, and the project sold out in less than 18 months.

Sixteen new luxury condominiums on Cashio Street in the Pico-Robertson district of Los Angeles were designed especially for the neighborhood's observant Jewish inhabitants. The three-bedroom units sold for $600,000 and up, attracting most buyers through flyers distributed at religious institutions and kosher markets and restaurants. An optional kosher amenities package includes dual dishwashers, counters, and sinks to accommodate separate preparation of meat and dairy products; ovens, refrigerators, and lighting that function with electrical timers to avoid having to operate switches during Shabbat, the Jewish Sabbath; and a specially designed *netila* hand-washing station.

Avoiding Litigation

Condominium development is fraught with the risk of litigation, but ways to minimize the risk exist. Aggregation is the primary culprit in condominium risk. Aggregate risk is caused by the inherent duplicative design and construction of condominium buildings. When something goes wrong in the design or construction of condominiums, the flaw is likely repeated throughout all units. As a result, negligible issues that may not have been pursued by one owner can now be addressed in a

Zocalo's buyers were attracted by Legorreta + Legorreta's design and an innovative Web site featuring photos and floor plans for individual units.
Lourdes Legorreta

First-time buyers, parents of Vanderbilt University students, and empty nesters were all attracted to the short commute and low-maintenance lifestyle of 807 Eighteenth in midtown Nashville. Alexa Bach

Buyer incentives at Kensington Park in Richfield, Minnesota, included free 42-inch flat-screen televisions, granite countertop upgrades, and monetary promotions to help with upgrades or closing costs. Sam Newberg

The Rise of the Nontraditional Household

The face of American households is undergoing a dramatic change, one that the multifamily housing industry is working to accommodate. The traditional family—married couples with children—is slowly declining in number, while households made up of single persons living alone, singles living together, and married couples without children are growing rapidly. Those three groups will account for 90 percent of the net new household growth projected by 2010, according to U.S. Census Bureau figures. What is different about the new household demographics is the sheer quantity of nontraditional arrangements.

Between 2000 and 2010, the number of childless couples and the number of singles living alone are both expected to increase by approximately 5 million, and the number of unrelated singles living together is expected to rise by about half a million. Meantime, the number of families with children is projected to rise by only 76,000 and the number of single-parent households is anticipated to remain stagnant. Indeed, by 2020, families consisting of two parents with children are expected to constitute only one household of every five.

Changing demographics and changing tastes will place a premium on the ability of developers and builders to build in flexibility and make adjustments. If a complex consists of two-bedroom condominiums and the market changes, the capacity to convert to efficiencies and lofts is essential.

Designing for Differences

"We believe people today are seeking a lifestyle, whether urban or suburban," observes George Currens, a principal with Irvine, California–based Style Interior Design. They are buying a particular environment, he explains, one composed of unit design, amenities, locale, and the visual impact an entire project can provide. If they are drawn to city living, whether they are young or middle aged, people have in common a desire to mix with other people, Currens believes. To accommodate this need, his firm designs spaces that provide the opportunity to meet others in fairly intimate settings, such as clubhouses and Internet cafés.

Some developers try to figure out exactly how many units of each type to build in a project by nailing the market precisely. Such precision is especially difficult with two-bedroom units, he explains, which are either "splits" for roommates or "tandems" for couples. Because two single people looking for housing together may also be a couple (male and female or same sex), the number of prospects who are single

Mostly empty nesters were attracted to the Palmolive, an ultraluxury condominium building on Chicago's Magnificent Mile. Draper and Kramer does not tell developers much about the appropriate ratio of splits to tandems.

Too much variety among units can also cause problems. For the agent, showing a customer every choice takes a lot of time. For the customer, too many choices can cause confusion and uncertainty. "There's a tipping point between having enough [choices] and so many that there's choice overload," says Daniel Gehman, an associate principal of Thomas C. Cox Architects in Irvine.

Targeting the Market

Currens maintains that developers have a number of misconceptions and frequently make a number of missteps in marketing housing to nontraditional households. In targeting one group or another, he says, some make the mistake of assuming everyone in that population is the same. In fact, he says, each subset, such as gays or 25-year-olds, contains a wide range of preferences, attitudes, and lifestyles, and marketing can no longer afford to go after only people in each group who constitute the majority and ignore the rest.

"We're seeing baby boomers who have no interest in Sun City," Currens says. Those individuals do not want to live in a retirement community or even be identified as seniors. Smart builders, he says, no longer segregate them into age-restricted communities, but rather have begun to integrate those individuals into other communities by building multifamily or single-family housing that stresses accessibility.

People do not always act their age. It is a misconception to think that only the young will be interested in urban projects. In marketing urban locations, Currens says, developers need to remember that "empty nesters may want that hip and cool activity as much as a 25-year-old." Furthermore, they are more apt to have the disposable income to afford intown living. What should be targeted is lifestyle, not age, he elaborates.

Reprinted with permission from *Multifamily Trends*, Summer 2005, published by the Urban Land Institute.

class action suit, allowing homeowners to share the effort and expense of filing a claim or suit. This possibility leads to a higher frequency and severity of condominium claims.

To manage risks, take the following steps:

» Organize the appropriate type of business entity. Determine the best business entity for the project and then periodically monitor its conduct to ensure that all corporate formalities are followed. These monitoring expenses are relatively small, and such actions and records will prove extremely helpful if a plaintiff tries to hold the developer personally liable for a mishap.

» Carefully prepare the condominium offering statement. The condominium offering statement is used by the developer to promote sales, but it can also serve as the basis for a misrepresentation claim by the individual unit owner or the future condominium association. A real estate attorney specializing in condominium development can clarify vague sections of the statement and confirm that any disclosures required by the state's condominium act are present. Offering statements need to include any covenants, conditions, and restrictions placed on the condominium and provide accurate estimates of condominium assessments necessary to cover the cost of operations, maintenance, insurance premiums, and reserves. The declaration is an opportunity for risk management and loss prevention if the development team is involved early enough in the project to provide input to the drafting of the document.

» Iron out the details before executing contracts. Upfront attention to detail and design decisions will enable the developer to select professionals, materials, and insurance that best suit its needs, avoiding later problems. At this point, it is also important to confirm that the primary contractor, subcontractor, and other professionals are properly insured and licensed in the state. Furthermore, the contracts must specifically deal with warranty liability and statutes of limitations and should encourage cooperative dispute resolution with the condominium owners.

» Hire an experienced construction superintendent. The construction superintendent needs to be willing to supervise workers and teach new building techniques. On-site training and education for contractors and workers may be necessary.

» Clearly define the parties' roles and obtain adequate insurance coverage. Architects design the plans and specifications for the project and also perform site visits during construction. The developer decides whether the scope of inspections

Located in the heart of Orlando, Florida, Baldwin Park (top), once a naval training center, is now a 1,100-acre vibrant community of residences, businesses, schools, and parks. Before new construction could begin, the developer dismantled and recycled 256 buildings, 200 miles of underground utilities, and 25 miles of roads. Debi Harbin

At buildout, Baldwin Park will house about 10,000 residents in 4,100 homes—including apartments, townhomes, condominiums, cottages, and custom-built homes—and 6,000 people will work in offices and stores in the project. Parks and lakes will cover the remaining 450 acres, nearly 40 percent of the community property. Debi Harbin

Managing the Unexpected

Since 1995, when the U.S. Environmental Protection Agency (EPA) established the brownfields initiative, brownfields across the nation began disappearing from the landscape as their revitalization became economically viable. The EPA program, which provides grants and loans for environmental assessment, cleanup, and job training, spurred new interest in brownfield cleanup by state and local governments as officials began realizing the economic, aesthetic, and tax benefits of restoring value to idle, unproductive, and underused real estate.

Consequently, many state and local governments have upped the ante, offering a variety of brownfield redevelopment incentives and policy changes to bait developer interest. New Jersey, for example, has implemented measures to limit liability for developers revitalizing brownfield sites and provides tax incentives to pay 75 percent of cleanup costs. Ohio allows developers to pay taxes on the old property value for 15 years after a brownfield site has been redeveloped. The state also implemented a program to expedite the environmental review process, which guarantees developers a turnaround of no more than 60 days. And Missouri provides tax credits up to 100 percent of a project's cleanup costs, depending on its calculated worth in terms of economic impact.

As a result, hundreds of contaminated sites large and small have been reclaimed for a variety of uses—retail, housing, office space, and parks—and many more are under development or in the planning stages. But there are still plenty more to go around: the EPA estimates that the nation's 150 years of disregard for the impact of industrial and commercial activities on land resources have given rise to an estimated 450,000 brownfields nationwide.

Although well-located brownfields in urban infill areas present opportunities to add value and reap profits, most developers are reluctant to plunge into territory where the only certainty is encountering the unknown. "Taking a corner of uptown that's an industrial mess and converting it to an upscale location is no small task," says Woods. "That's why so few people in this industry are willing to take on projects like this."

Brownfield projects are more complex and present greater risk exposure than greenfield sites, but they also have greater profit margin potential. "There are opportunities to buy properties for pennies on the dollar and sell for as much as 50 to 60 times what is spent on the project," Egan contends, but he admits that for every success, there is a failure because a developer did not do his or her homework. He says that the biggest mistake developers make is going into the process without enough leverage to see the project through. "You have to come to the table prepared, know the economics of the situation—upfront and planning costs, how long you can sit on your money, what can be made, and what must be spent to make a reasonable profit," maintains Egan.

Both Egan and Jim Hughes, an environmental attorney in the Los Angeles office of McKenna, Aldridge & Long LLC, suggest that leveraging a brownfield project with borrowed money is a tricky and risky business, because the lender's clock is ticking and delays are inevitable due to environmental reviews and signoffs. "The entire profit relies on bringing land to positive value from negative value," points out Hughes. "These projects [take] two to three times as long as the typical project—making the permitting process look like child's play. Stitching together both the real estate and environmental requirements takes patience and money, so it's best to have money partners and investors."

One way to cut red tape and time delays is to file a negative declaration for a voluntary environmental assessment, says Hughes, explaining that this allows the developer to conduct the engineering assessment without governmental oversight, and shortens the timeline by nine to 18 months. A voluntary action may enable a developer to secure a "consent not to sue" and avoid a forced cleanup, which is particularly beneficial for owners involved in creating the brownfield condition in the first place. It also provides an opportunity for the owner to profit from restoring the property's value and/or full potential. One example of a voluntary cleanup is the brownfield redevelopment project planned by Boeing Realty on Boeing's 238-acre former aircraft manufacturing site in Long Beach, California, which is being replaced with Douglas Park, a mixed-use community featuring 1,400 homes and 3.3 million square feet of commercial space.

With advances in environmental technology, experts agree that most brownfield issues are quite manageable, but a project's success rests on both real estate basics and the developer's ability to assemble an experienced team of experts to provide legal, environmental, liability, and financial expertise.

When selecting a brownfield site for redevelopment, "Don't ignore the basics of real estate: location, location, location," says environmental lawyer Stuart Lieberman, a principal at Princeton, New Jersey–based Lieberman & Blecher, P.C. "If a property is a dog, it will bark and have fleas whether it's contaminated or not. Keep in mind that a good location

has infrastructure associated with it and is feasible for the proposed use."

Hughes suggests that developers attempt only those brownfield projects that are located in familiar territory, which helps in anticipating variables that may arise. Moreover, K. Robert "Bobby" Turner, managing partner for Los Angeles–based Canyon-Johnson Capital, which has done brownfield redevelopment projects in urban infill locations throughout the nation, points out that environmental regulations vary greatly from state to state and city to city. He therefore advises developers to secure the services of professionals—legal, environmental, and insurance—with a national perspective, especially if the site is located in unfamiliar territory.

It goes without saying that environmental liability insurance is a developer's safest hedge against entering a brownfield "twilight zone." But David Sterling, an independent insurance consultant with New York–based Sterling & Sterling, Inc., cautions against jumping into the game without a coach. "There's no cookie-cutter policy," he says, stressing the importance of involving an insurance consultant with knowledge of brownfield liability issues. Sterling explains that brownfield liability coverage is a patchwork based on a site's unique history and circumstances, which must be defined in the policy to ensure protection against the unexpected.

Liability insurance rates vary according to state laws, the size of the project, and the extent of documentation available on the site's environmental status, but a policy typically costs between $50,000 and $100,000, according to Sterling. Noting that insurers require documentation that the state has approved the environmental assessment and cleanup plan, he suggests also having an attorney assess the risk based on the environmental reports to provide the broker ammunition to use in negotiating the best rate with an underwriter.

Reprinted with permission from *Urban Land*, June 2005, published by the Urban Land Institute.

After Hurricane Katrina swept through New Orleans, the Bakery's unit owners association quickly restored landscaping, cleared common areas of debris, and facilitated unit inspection for insurance purposes. Each owner was individually liable for damage within condominium homes. B. Kriesler

should be as the clerk of works, the owner's on-site representative on a day-to-day basis, or in accordance with other guidelines. The developer must ensure that all design professionals, contractors, and subcontractors obtain adequate insurance as determined by the nature, size, and scope of the project. For assistance or guidelines in defining the roles, responsibilities, and liabilities of the architect, the contractors, and the owner, see American Institute of Architects (AIA) General Conditions of the Contract for Construction, document A201 as revised in 1997.[6] A201 was written by legal and insurance experts in consultation with experienced architects. The document addresses the owner-architect agreement, certificates of insurance, the architect's insurance, insurance claims, and construction bonds, among many other topics. The A201, however, will need to be customized by the developer's attorney.

» Implement a quality assurance strategy. Hold regular quality assurance meetings and develop a quality measurement system. Bowron, Latta & Wasden, P.C., a law firm based in Mobile, Alabama, recommends obtaining verification in writing from manufacturers that materials—especially windows, exterior cladding systems, and roofs—meet building envelope and code requirements. Specialized materials might require retaining an insured, specialized consultant to oversee and/or approve installation. Make certain to obtain a valid certified warranty on products or work before issuing the last check to each manufacturer or supplier.

» Verify the building code. Check with the local governmental entity responsible for enforcing the building code in case the code is being updated or rewritten. Any changes need to be incorporated into the design process as soon as possible.

» Oversee a smooth transition to the new condominium UOA. The developer needs to ensure a smooth transfer of responsibilities to the new unit owners association, including establishing the initial UOA board. This transition should include retaining the services of an experienced condominium management company. Also, review the completed building and all construction documents to certify that the condominium offering statement is still accurate.

» Make the owners' maintenance responsibilities very clear. Clearly list all maintenance responsibilities of the UOA, including funding for the maintenance program. This step might include compiling a maintenance manual with information from all product manufacturers. Then limit or prohibit developer liability if the UOA does not follow through with suggested routine care. In addition, the developer should maintain an accurate paper trail regarding warranty issues, homeowner complaints, and the developer's response to work requests.

Condominium Associations

Making the transition from developer to homeowner control is a multistage process that begins with the preparation of community association documents. These documents, including the articles of incorporation (when required), the declaration, and the bylaws, are prepared early in the development process and are sometimes required during the approval process. After those documents are prepared, the community association budget can be established. The developer typically controls the decisions of the association throughout the construction and conveyance process but can choose to involve future homeowners to ensure the project meets expectations. Meet-and-greet sessions, welcome packages, periodic association meetings, association newsletters, and Web forums can create a sense of community and address potential issues before the association is controlled by homeowners. To manage community input, the developer-controlled association can set up advisory homeowner committees. These committees serve as transition teams. They are usually elected by homeowners and keep all owners up to date regarding the schedule for turnover of responsibility, budget process, and contractual obligations. Many states have laws mandating a specific process for turnover from developer to owner control. In this case, the governing documents should reflect the required process.

IDI Group Companies, a developer based in Arlington, Virginia, uses an extremely effective model to transfer control from the developer to the association. As soon as 25 percent of the new homeowners move into a building, IDI conducts a resident orientation, establishes resident advisory committees, and hands out a notebook dictating the community association's structure. IDI typically creates five committees—Activities, Budget and Finance, Building and Grounds, Communications, and Rules and Covenants. When almost half of the homeowners have moved into the building, IDI holds an election for two positions on the condominium association's board. At that time, IDI also establishes an Engineering Warranty Committee made up of homeowners with engineering or re-

lated skills to cooperatively select an independent engineering firm to evaluate the project for warranty purposes. A reserve study is performed to guarantee that the owners are satisfied that the developer provided enough funds for the condominium association. All of IDI's upfront effort facilitates the election of the full owner's board. By then, the homeowners are familiar with each other and the budget, building structure, and maintenance of the property. The Activities Committee immediately schedules "Get to Know Your Neighbor" events to welcome all new residents to the neighborhood.

Notes

1. Median new home price data are adjusted for inflation. Provided by National Association of Realtors.

2. Median prices estimated by National Association of Realtors.

3. Secretary of the Interior's Standards and Guidelines for Archeology and Historic Preservation. effective September 19, 1983. Available at www.cr.nps .gov/local-law/arch_stnds_0.htm.

4. Americans with Disabilities Act Technical Assistance Letter, the Honorable Charles S. Robb, United States Senate, Doc. no. 280, March 10, 1993. Available at www.usdoj.gov/crt/foia/tal280.txt.

5. For a more detailed discussion of market analysis, see Adrienne Schmitz and Deborah L. Brett, *Real Estate Market Analysis: A Case Study Approach*, (Washington, D.C.: ULI–the Urban Land Institute, 2001).

6. AIA General Conditions of the Contract for Construction, document A201 as revised in 1997. Available at www.aia.org.

Condominium associations manage the use and maintenance of common areas within a community. John Sutton, Sharon Risendorph

CASE STUDIES

Each in its own way, the ten case studies in this book address the opportunities and challenges of condominium development. They include projects within suburban master-planned communities, urban adaptive use, conversions, and small-scale new construction. All projects are substantially or completely built out. The cases illustrate why the deal worked, why the location appealed to the developer, how the developer determined the target market and subsequently catered to it, and how the developer ensured a profit. The case studies also emphasize the innovative strategies the developers used to stand out from the competition. These winning strategies include green building, exceptional location, exclusive amenities, and creative design. Several projects highlight how the developer was able to maintain affordability in light of escalating construction costs and market demand.

THE BAKERY

New Orleans, Louisiana

The Consumer's Biscuit Company building, a four-story, 80,000-square-foot structure located in the Warehouse District of New Orleans, was vacant by the time HRI purchased it in 1992. That year, HRI, a New Orleans–based development firm specializing in adaptive use of historic buildings, converted the building—which it named the Bakery—to 66 rental apartments. A market study by real estate consultant Herbert/Smolkin Associates accurately projected that the building would be 90 percent leased within nine months of its opening.

In 2003, HRI again converted the building, this time to condominiums. The conversion fit HRI's mission, which has been to revitalize cities by creating diverse, vibrant, and sustainable communities. Its approach to redevelopment is holistic, incorporating community needs, historic preservation, and community and economic revitalization. HRI employs staff professionals in all areas of development, including architecture, financing, construction, and residential management.

The Site

The city of New Orleans is geographically defined by districts. The Warehouse District, where the Bakery is located, is bounded by the Central Business District, which borders the city's most famous attraction, the French Quarter, and the Lower Garden District, known for its splendid Victorian single-family houses and gardens. The Crescent City Connection in the Warehouse District links the area by bridge over the Mississippi River to Highway 90, a major thoroughfare to southern Louisiana and beyond.

The Bakery is two blocks from the convention center and Riverwalk shopping complex, both of which straddle the Mississippi River. Adjacent to the Bakery is a hotel that was converted from a historic building, a restaurant, and other historic residential buildings, including HRI's 132-unit Federal Fiber Mills condominium.

The Developer

Since its founding in 1982 by Pres Kabacoff and the late Edward B. Boettner, HRI has completed 36 large-scale projects nationwide. Among them are 2,904 apartment units, 2,738 hotel rooms, and office and retail space, at a cost of $907 million. Federal Fiber Mills, which HRI converted to luxury apartments, launched the transformation of this industrial area on the Mississippi River waterfront—previously the site of abandoned and decaying warehouses—to an economically thriving residential community. In about 20 years, the Warehouse District became a vibrant community where residents live, work, and

play, a trio of benefits that emerged as adaptive use became a way to revitalize cities.

HRI subsequently replicated its recipe for economic revitalization of decaying urban areas elsewhere in Louisiana— Baton Rouge, Hammond, Houma, Lafayette, New Iberia, and Shreveport—where adaptive use was a linchpin of economic revitalization. The company became identified with adaptive use projects in other cities as well, converting hotels, schools, hospitals, and warehouses into viable living, commercial, and retail space in Fort Worth, Texas; Omaha, Nebraska; St. Louis, Missouri, and elsewhere. HRI's portfolio today totals more than $1 billion in renovated properties. By the time the company converted the 71-year-old Consumer's Biscuit Company building, HRI was established in the area of adaptive use.

When HRI saw the adaptive use market in New Orleans drying up, the company concentrated on other housing oppor-

Six units replaced four huge brick ovens, each 27 feet tall and about 18 feet deep. These units are now two stories, with spiral staircases leading to bedrooms with barrel-vaulted brick ceilings. HRI

The atrium's glass ceiling provides sunlight to the interior windows of each unit. HRI

tunities. It made a substantial investment in affordable and market-rate mixed-use development in a project called River Garden, formerly the site of the 70-acre St. Thomas public housing project. The company also pursued conversions in other urban centers and new construction in urban New Orleans, and it promotes mixed-use development as a means of providing housing and repopulating the city in the wake of Hurricane Katrina in September 2005.

Development Process

Built in 1920, the Bakery building housed New Orleans's first mass-production, assembly-line bakery. Mammoth ovens, two stories high, presented an important architectural challenge in the adaptive use of the building. When the building was initially converted to apartments, it yielded 47,465 square feet of net rentable space. That remained unchanged when the building was converted to condominiums.

The district's location fostered walkable urban living, which Kabacoff felt was essential in reviving the depressed urban center. The neighborhood boasts upscale lofts, mixed-income apartments and condominiums, galleries, hotels, and night-clubs. Within walking distance are such attractions as the National D-Day Museum, the Contemporary Arts Center, the Louisiana Children's Museum, and the Ogden Museum of Southern Art.

By 2003, several economic and social factors fueled the decision to convert the building from apartments to mid-priced condominiums. Low interest rates, market trends that made condominiums an attractive option for young professionals seeking proximity to the city's business district, empty nesters, and those seeking a low-maintenance second or vacation homes were contributing factors. So was the growing confidence among lenders in the Warehouse District's condominium market. Another major motivator was the city's Restoration Abatement Tax Program, which the Louisiana state legislature passed in 1983 as an economic stimulus to encourage redevelopment of warehouses and other commercial structures into multifamily properties in downtown and historic districts. The program was expiring, putting an end to a renewable five-year deferred property tax assessment that normally would be assessed for improvements, thereby leaving owners with limited options—convert their building on their own or sell to condominium developers when their tax break expired.

A 2004 report by the Real Estate Market Data Center at the University of New Orleans revealed that the conversion of downtown warehouses into apartments and lofts added 3,000 new households to the Warehouse District, far ahead of the French Quarter, which added about 1,000 condominium units in the past several years. Both areas had occupancy rates of 97 percent, compared with 94 percent overall in New Orleans, and sales prices then reaching $200 to $350 per square foot in the Warehouse District and $400 to $425 in the French Quarter. "It was important because sales added to the tax-payer base in the city, thereby making the city stronger, which was an important factor to HRI. The conversion also allowed us to upgrade and preserve another historic building," said Eddie Boettner, chief administrative officer, cochairman of the board of directors, and son of Kabacoff's late partner.

Financing

During the building's apartment tenure, HRI jointly owned the Bakery with its tax credit investor and limited partner Dover Historic Properties Fund. In 2003, HRI purchased the apartment building from the partnership for $4.7 million with the intention of converting it to condominiums. This plan provided

an exit strategy for the limited partner and an opportunity to take advantage of market conditions.

The condominium conversion, which represented a $7.4 million acquisition and renovation, was financed through a loan for purchase from AmSouth Bank, with which HRI had an existing relationship. AmSouth provided a first mortgage of $3.65 million, secured by the property through a revolving $1.8 million line of credit for the upgrades to the kitchens, bathrooms, and common areas. HRI's cash equity contribution was $1.28 million. The difference between the overall costs and financing sources (approximately $700,000) was covered by the sales proceeds of the first few units.

Buyers secured their own permanent financing on their condominium units. AmSouth underwrote the continuation of the property as rental units as a backup to the condominium conversion/sale program in the event condominium sales failed and the building remained rental only.

In 1998, operating expenses on the building were $4,170 per unit annually ($275,220 overall) and were expected to grow 3 percent a year. As a result of the city's tax abatement program, property taxes remained frozen until July 31, 2002. The operating expenses included a reserve fund annual set-aside for the 66 units at $150 a unit, or $9,900 a year, to cover the costs of extraordinary capital expenses such as roof replacement at the end of its useful life.

Planning, Design, and Construction

Structurally, the condominium conversion of the units was limited to renovating existing kitchens and bathrooms. A market analysis by HRI determined that to make units salable, specific upgrades would be necessary. Unit upgrades included granite countertops, stainless steel appliances, new cabinets, and ceramic kitchen and bathroom tile, which enabled HRI to sell the apartments for $140,000 to $267,000. The common areas were also upgraded, including carpeting, new paint, and light fixtures, and the rooftop pool and cabana were refurbished. The roof was replaced, windows were reglazed, and the brick was tuck pointed—the process that repairs mortar between bricks to prevent cracking, flaking, and other disintegration. Total costs of construction and related soft costs above and beyond acquisition of the units averaged $37,763 per unit.

Pedestrian entrance to the building is through a secured gate that opens onto a central skylit atrium, an enclosed stained and scored concrete and landscaped courtyard with the original wood beams exposed through the four-story building. An elevator reaches the second, third, and fourth floors and hallways that access the units. Unlike other HRI adaptive use projects, no salvageable structures or machinery, such as boilers or sewing machines, could be used for design elements in the form of found-object art, which HRI uses, where possible, at its other properties.

The building's unique architectural feature is the design of six units that replaced four huge brick ovens, each 27 feet tall and about 18 feet deep. The large Ferris wheel devices that once carried trays of crackers from the baking area to the boxing process were removed. In the conversion to apartments, two units are two stories, with spiral staircases leading to bedrooms with barrel-vaulted brick ceilings. Preserved were 27-foot-tall brick walls. The remaining units include one-, two-, and three-bedroom models featuring 13- to 18-foot ceilings, huge windows, and the original hardrock maple floors.

The architectural style is turn-of-the-century industrial (light brick) masonry and heavy timber construction. Amenities include a rooftop pool, a ground-floor fitness center, and a landscaped atrium with a fountain. There are 56 parking spaces for the 66 units, including 24 garage and 32 adjacent surface-lot spaces. The building has exterior views from all four sides, including a view of the Crescent City Connection, Mississippi River, Federal Fiber Mills, and downtown cityscape.

Marketing, Management, Tenants, and Performance

HRI, which was solely responsible for development, sales (through a third-party broker), and property management, capitalized on the robust demand for owner-occupied units in the Warehouse District and favorable market conditions in general by converting the rental apartments to mid-priced condominiums. To determine market demand, HRI interviewed real estate agents and brokers, and analyzed sales and listings data as well as trends from the Multiple Listing Service and other private sources.

The Bakery was an ideal housing product for professionals, most of whom were first-time homebuyers. It is near main arterials, public transportation, and the business district, and the units were affordably priced. HRI analyzed its existing rental leases to determine the length of time remaining on each of them. Whenever possible, HRI exercised the 30-day termination clause in its leases; in those leases without a cancellation clause, HRI was required to wait out the full term of the lease. Throughout the process, HRI's intention was to maximize the opportunity for a continued revenue stream and maintain the highest rental occupancy possible during unit sales and renovations. As the units became available and went under contract to purchasers, the company took 75 days to

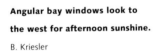

Angular bay windows look to the west for afternoon sunshine. B. Kriesler

Indoor vegetation and fountains create a private oasis for residents. B. Kriesler

Most buyers were young professionals, in many cases first-time homebuyers, attracted by the proximity to main arterials, public transportation, and the business district. HRI

close. This time was spent finalizing the individual upgrades as well as obtaining the purchasers' financing.

For its targeted condominium buyer market, HRI retained a mostly small, one-bedroom-unit size of less than 500 square feet that initially sold for about $108,000, with prices escalating for the larger one- and two-bedroom units and 18 penthouses on the upper floors. The condominium fees start at $150 and average $200 per month as the unit square footage increases.

To market the units, HRI first offered them to existing tenants, hosting two kickoff wine and cheese receptions for them and enticing them with a 14-day exclusive offer to purchase their units at a 10 percent discount off the public sales price. About 15 percent of residents purchased units, which were offered either with or without the upgrades. The success of this approach led HRI to extend a similar purchase offer to residents of its Cotton Mill property when it started converting that project into condominiums in 2004.

HRI had a preexisting relationship with New Orleans–based Thomas Long Corporate Communications and hired the company to conceptualize and design advertising products. Marketing products for the Bakery played off the building's history. According to Boettner, the most successful sales vehicle was word-of-mouth communication.

After the tenant base was exhausted, advertisements were placed in the city's main newspaper, the *Times Picayune*, specialty print media, HRI's Web site, and billboards placed in high traffic areas close to the site. Within 11 months of closing on the purchase of the building, all units but the largest were sold.

Experience Gained

The Bakery represented HRI's smallest condominium project and the first conversion in a decade.

» **Space and style.** "We found out that what was most desirable in the market was an open floor plan, and such materials as granite countertops and stainless steel appliances," said Selim Berkol, director of finance.

» **Speaking the same language.** "We also learned from a financing as well as marketing perspective that while we looked at pricing the units on a per square footage basis, most condominium purchasers did not. Especially in the first-time homebuyer segment, their interest was the overall amount of money they are being asked to spend on a unit. There is a price point for them. If they have found a building that they want to live in with the amenities they desire and the ultimate advantage of living close to downtown, they are not so much concerned about square footage as they are about the overall price," he said.

» **Responsive pricing.** "We also learned to look to the market when pricing different units, pricing larger units at less per square foot than smaller units."

» **Active marketing.** HRI learned how to market the units to their renters, particularly those who may be purchasing for the short term, advising them of the financial benefits of purchasing their unit and taking advantage of an active condominium market.

Effect of Hurricane Katrina

Hurricane Katrina was the first category 5 hurricane of the 2005 Atlantic hurricane season and the most destructive and most costly natural disaster in the history of the United States. It was the third-most-powerful storm of the season, behind Hurricane Wilma and Hurricane Rita, and the sixth-strongest storm ever recorded in the Atlantic basin. Katrina dropped to a strong category 3 storm (125 mile per hour winds) before making its second landfall on the morning of August 29 along the central Gulf Coast. Several sections of the levee system protecting New Orleans from Lake Pontchartrain and the Mississippi River collapsed, allowing water to quickly flood most of the low-lying city. Heavy winds and storm surge further destroyed the city. Estimates of Katrina's damage range from $200 billion to $300 billion, at least double that of Hurricane Andrew, previously the most expensive hurricane.

HRI Properties responded as quickly as possible to the storm, setting up a temporary office in Houma, Louisiana, and asking all of its employees to report to work as soon as their family situation was stable. HRI opened several of its apartment communities in North Carolina, Missouri, and Shreveport, Louisiana, for hurricane evacuees. Condominium owners and apartment renters were able to view the status of their homes through periodic updates and photographs on HRI's Web site.

The Bakery, as well as most of the Warehouse District, is located on what New Orleans defines as "high ground" and therefore suffered minimally from the storm. Strong winds blew out several windows, and negligible damage to the roof and subsequent water damage occurred, but the property was not harmed by floodwater or looters, as occurred in other portions of the city.

Owners were able to return to their homes on October 3, 2005, when the landscaping and common areas were cleared of debris, all utilities were functioning, and the roof was repaired. Some damage to individual units remained; each condominium had to be inspected separately for insurance purposes. September and October condominium payments were due upon occupancy; however, because of the circumstances, no late fees were assessed. The Bakery's management team arranged for a third-party contractor to clean refrigerators, at the owner's cost, for those unable to return to New Orleans by October 10, 2005.

Hurricane Katrina was the most destructive and most costly natural disaster in the history of the United States. Cade Martin

Project Data: The Bakery

www.bakerycondo.net

Land Use Information

Site area: 30,100 square feet

Total dwelling units planned: 65

Total dwelling units completed: 66 (one large unit was
   divided into two one-bedroom condominiums)

Parking: 32 surface spaces/24 garage spaces

Land Use Plan

	Square Feet	Percentage of Site
Attached residential	20,840	71
Parking garage	9,260	29
Total	30,100	100

Residential Unit Information

Unit Type (Bedroom/ Bath)	Average Unit Size (Square Feet)	Number of Units Built	Average Sales Prices
1/1	575	52	$125,000
2/1	1,095	12	$222,300
3/2	1,980	2	$346,500

Development Cost Information

Site acquisition cost	$ 4,700,000
Site improvement and construction costs	2,055,000
Soft costs	790,000
Total development cost	**$ 7,545,000**

Development Schedule

Site purchased:	May 2003
Planning started:	January 2003
Construction started (conversion):	May 2003
Sales started:	May 2003
First closing:	August 2003
Phase 1 completed (conversion):	August 2004
Project completed and sold out:	February 2005

Developer, Site Planner, and Architect

HRI Properties

New Orleans, Louisiana

www.hrihci.com

Two-bedroom, one-bath floor plan. HRI

807 EIGHTEENTH

Nashville, Tennessee

The first for-sale residential project in Nashville, Tennessee's Midtown neighborhood in approximately 20 years, 807 Eighteenth was also the first endeavor for Nashville-based M2H Group. Convinced of the urban neighborhood's historic significance and high-quality location—sandwiched between Music Row and Vanderbilt University—the pioneering firm successfully broke Midtown's residential development drought with this new urbanist infill project that subsequently sold out while still in construction.

The project blends a modern brownstone streetscape with "refined funky" condominiums in the rear of the building. The project is oriented to the street with 46 condominium units in a stacked townhome configuration over 52 underground parking spaces. Creative building design achieved the planned density of 92 dwelling units per acre, while specially chosen architectural features—including an interior courtyard, oversized windows, and exterior walkways on upper floors—create a more intimate ambience than standard mid-rise buildings.

The Site

The project is located in the heart of the Midtown neighborhood in Nashville, Tennessee. The neighborhood is named for its location, nestled between downtown Nashville, filled with live music venues and professional sports facilities, and the historic, parklike campus of Vanderbilt University. Midtown is also home to Music Row—the heart of the country music recording industry.

Midtown was originally settled as a residential enclave outside the downtown trade district, and the residential fabric is still evident in the early 20th-century homes lining 18th Avenue and the surrounding blocks. Most of the remaining structures are now used as business offices for both the music industry and various professional companies.

To the east of the project lies Music Row, with corporate headquarters, small music recording offices, and songwriters' studios. Music Row runs north-south, parallel to 18th Avenue along a one-way couplet traffic pattern down 16th and 17th avenues. Providing easy access to downtown as well as the shopping districts to the south of Midtown, Music Row is a major thoroughfare in Nashville.

To the south of the site, commercial uses give way to residential uses, and then Hillsboro Village, an eclectic neighborhood shopping area and town center.

To the west of the site is Vanderbilt University's 330-acre campus. More than just a world-renowned academic institution, Vanderbilt includes a first-class hospital system, research facilities, and a Veterans Administration hospital within its

807 Eighteenth was the first endeavor for Nashville-based M2H Group. Breaking Midtown's 20-year drought in for-sale residential development, the 46-unit building is sandwiched between Music Row and Vanderbilt University. Aerial Innovations of TN, Inc.

The square site lent itself to a hollowed-out building configuration with a central courtyard and elevator tower (above). This design provides each residence with light and air on at least two sides and access to the central open space.
Alexa Bach

Architectural features—including an interior courtyard, oversized windows, and exterior walkways on upper floors—create a more intimate ambience than is found in standard mid-rise buildings.

Aerial Innovations of TN, Inc.

boundaries. In addition to being Nashville's largest employer, Vanderbilt, with its green campus, offers a quiet respite within the city. The university was designated a national arboretum in 1988, and the Peabody section of campus is a registered National Historic Landmark with buildings that date to Vanderbilt's founding in 1873.

To the north and northwest, the street grid is interrupted by the Midtown business district, oriented on the diagonal Division Street. This area is predominantly occupied by service retail establishments, including more than 42 restaurants that are within walking distance of 807 Eighteenth.

Three individual residential lots were assembled to yield the half acre that became 807 Eighteenth's site. The soils are thin—two to three feet of topsoil over hard blue-granite bedrock. The topography slopes gently to the west, dropping ten to 12 feet across the 150-foot-deep property. Little vegetation was present because the site previously was home to an empty music studio, the burned-out shell of a house, and an

open gravel parking lot between the two buildings. An alley splits the block between 18th and 19th avenues and provides rear-entry access to 807 Eighteenth.

The Developer

M2H Group was founded in 2001 by Marty Heflin, who had previously built almost 1,000 multifamily units in Nashville. The small firm now includes a partner, Bob Springer, and has support staff and offices in Nashville and Denver, Colorado. It focuses on community needs, pledging to pursue "organic development" that is sensitive to the site and its neighborhood. In lieu of a "cookie cutter" approach to development that seeks to force a product that was produced elsewhere onto a site, M2H is committed to allowing the site and the neighborhood to steer the design. The company asserts that it pursues responsible development and, as a result, M2H will look to the future with new initiatives, including green building and transit-oriented development strategies.

Development Process

The nationwide housing boom of the early 2000s injected life into Nashville's residential real estate market. In that time, a record number of homes have been constructed and sold, many catering to an influx of migrants moving from high-priced coastal metropolitan areas to middle Tennessee. Nashville's home values have heated up but are far from the explosive markets of the east and west coasts. Median home price in the Nashville area has risen 14 percent between 2002 and 2005 to $154,000, compared to the national median home price that has risen 19 percent to $188,000. This influx of homebuyers is part of an overall population increase in Nashville, which has grown by 7.4 percent since 2000. Nashville's well-diversified economy led the way to creating job opportunities even in the recession of 2001 to 2002.

With metropolitan Nashville's growing population and geographic constraints for suburban sprawl, commutes to its north and south have lengthened since 2000. In response, M2H spent time looking for a walkable neighborhood situated close to employment and entertainment that would simplify the lives of commuters.

Planning for 807 Eighteenth began in 2003 when Nashville's condominium market was in its infancy. The developers honed their strategy using evidence from other markets showing that a percentage of the population prefers the simple, safe lifestyle alternative of multifamily housing when it is well located. M2H also saw the well-educated and well-paid population of Nashville as constituting an excellent market facing undersupply and pent-up demand.

Heflin identified the site for 807 Eighteenth and turned it over to Springer to create a development concept. The original site-design concepts and financials were literally sketched out on a napkin over a Sam Adams and kung pao chicken in a neighborhood Chinese restaurant. After refining the ideas using Excel spreadsheets to improve the layout and development of a pro forma, both partners agreed on the design and concept, and they decided to pursue the property for development.

The concept remained fairly constant once refined by M2H Group. A printout defining the arrangement and approximate unit sizes and configuration of the courtyard and parking was brought to the project architect, who provided construction documents for the project as it was ultimately built.

Condominiums were chosen for 807 Eighteenth to balance the product with the surrounding mixed-use neighborhood. Many six- to eight-story buildings are nearby, along with two- and three-story houses from the turn of the last century. For-sale product was chosen for both its character and value. M2H thought a small rental project would be hard to manage profitably and found the value in the marketplace was significantly higher for condominiums ($200 per square foot compared with $100 per square foot).

Approvals, Design, and Construction

The property was chosen specifically because the existing zoning and policy supported the planned use, density, and configuration. The reason was twofold: first, M2H tries to work with the community vision by implementing the policy and zoning already in place; second, this decision shortens the development cycle and removes entitlement risk. As a result, the approval process is whittled down to merely obtaining a building permit. In addition, the neighborhood supports the investment, encourages progress, and celebrates the new neighbors.

M2H Group first decided that to promote a walkable community the project should present a pedestrian-scale face to 18th Avenue. That concept drove the decision to create a modern brownstone or rowhouse facade with stacked townhomes right along the sidewalk and condominium flats behind.

The perfectly square site, for which a floor plate covering the entire square area was not desirable, immediately suggested a central courtyard or community space around which the flats were placed. The hollowed-out configuration provides each residence with light and air on at least two sides and access to the central area—though windows and openings are positioned so that none of the units is looking straight into another building or window. The site topography influenced the final design decision. The ten-to-12-foot slope across the 150-foot-deep property allowed a level of parking to be built under the building, covering almost the entire half acre. With alley access from the back, vehicle traffic or vehicle entrances would not interrupt the building line and streetscape.

The neighborhood is diverse in both land use and building type. No consistency exists between the corporate offices of national music companies and the small bungalow-style homes sitting between them. This diversity provided a large design palette, allowing M2H to relate easily to both mid- and high-rise buildings within a block from the site.

The architectural concept was a modern interpretation of a brownstone, and as a design motto, M2H Group coined the term "refined funky." The project's funkiness is seen in the light blue-green siding on the condominium buildings that abut the back of the brownstones. The silver-colored steel railings, walkways, and elevators provide a hint of urban industrial character, and several first-floor units have glass garage doors that open the living/dining room to the courtyards.

M2H Group originally planned to build two three-bedroom, 2.5-bathroom townhomes that would occupy all four floors on both streetfront corners of the project. After reassessing market demand, M2H Group decided to split those units into four two-bedroom, 2.5-bathroom units, each with two floors.

The interiors of the condominium units were designed to be open and inviting. Eight loft units have living areas with huge, 12-foot-high windows on 18-foot walls. These top-floor units, which M2H called sky lofts, commanded some of the highest prices per square foot. Many of the other units have steps separating the kitchen from the living areas. Bay windows and balconies offer views of downtown Nashville, Vanderbilt, and the Midtown district. Kitchens typically have open plans with islands separating dining and cooking space that maintain a spacious feel. The standard design package included environmentally friendly bamboo flooring, but buyers could upgrade to maple. The bedrooms include a creative twist. Instead of choosing to paint all walls, molding, and trim "builder beige," as is standard in most new condominium buildings, M2H Group chose a neutral, yet distinctive shade of purplish gray with black wood trim.

The walkable neighborhood has readily available and useful public transportation. The parking consists of 52 underground garage spaces, a ratio of 1.13 spaces per unit, or 0.8 spaces per bedroom. The parking meets requirements of the city of Nashville and Davidson County, which have urban zoning overlay provisions that reduce the parking requirement for infill residential projects.

The parking has been adequate from the market perspective as well. All 46 units and 52 spaces were sold before construction was finished. No homeowners, to M2H Group's knowledge, wanted a space but were unable to buy one.

Green building is a major priority for M2H Group. The company is continually brainstorming ideas for including green materials, technologies, and other pathways for lightening the environmental footprint of its buildings. Several green elements were incorporated into 807 Eighteenth, including the selection of an infill site, which is inherently green because it uses the existing infrastructure and resources. Additionally, the bamboo floors offered in the standard design package are an environmentally responsible choice because bamboo (which is actually grass, not wood) is a highly renewable resource, harvestable only four to six years after being planted. It also features naturally low moisture-absorption properties and is extremely durable.

From a site-work perspective, M2H Group saw the drainage system as the biggest opportunity to use green techniques.

Eight loft units have living areas with huge, 12-foot-high windows on 18-foot walls. Standard interior features include open kitchen plans with dining islands and bamboo flooring; many units have views from their balconies of downtown Nashville, Vanderbilt, and the Midtown district.
Aerial Innovations of TN, Inc.

M2H Group calls the design "refined funky." The project melds modern brownstone with light blue-green siding and silver-colored steel railings, walkways, and elevators to create an urban industrial character. Alexa Bach

M2H Group used a modern brownstone facade along 18th Street to promote a walkable community. Alexa Bach

Because 807 Eighteenth is in a highly urbanized area, site runoff has an immediate compounded effect on the local water quality, particularly in the Cumberland River, which bisects the city. M2H Group paved the parking spaces sheltered under the residential buildings but used pervious concrete in the areas where parking is exposed to weather. This material allows rainwater to percolate into the ground and filters vehicle discharge. All site and roof drainage was filtered to the edges of the project where the runoff is delivered to two bio-swale systems. The naturally draining bio-swales act both as a natural filter to trap particulates and as very small detention streams. The swales are lined with native plant material and are underlain with porous backfill, allowing maximum absorption into the groundwater as well as another opportunity to filter runoff. Excess drainage is discharged to the surface in much the same way as prior to development, but at lower velocity and volume.

Financing

The project cost just over $8.5 million to develop. The site was acquired for $850,000, and M2H spent another $775,000 on improvements. Construction cost $6 million, while soft costs—including architectural fees, legal expenses, financing, marketing, and other services—added another $900,000.

The principals of M2H Group are the general partners in the development entity, and construction financing was provided by the Nashville office of Alabama-based Regions Bank. The project's cost structure was 20 percent equity, 80 percent construction loan. Regions Bank required 50 percent presales to close on the loan and held an 80 percent loan-to-value ratio based on the appraised value of the building.

In deciding whether to pursue a project, M2H Group uses a hurdle rate of 20 percent profit on net income. If M2H Group does not foresee a project as able to provide at least a 20 percent profit, it will drop the project from consideration. This decision is based on M2H's philosophy that a fast "no" is much better than a drawn-out "maybe." The largest element of uncertainty for 807 Eighteenth was market risk, which was managed through structuring and timing of the deal. While most developers were using "reservation contracts" to secure financing, M2H required at least 5 percent of the purchase price as down payment. The equity funds came in upfront during the presale period, and the land contract was structured on an option basis so that closing was delayed until the presales were confirmed.

Marketing, Sales, and Buyer Profile

The marketing program for 807 Eighteenth included a consistent print campaign, signage at the site and in local restaurants and retail businesses, and an Internet presence, along with interspersed public relations statements announcing sales pace, move-in, completion, and milestone events such as groundbreaking and deck completion. 807 Eighteenth attracted a demographically diverse group of buyers, all drawn by the short commute and low-maintenance lifestyle. First-time buyers, including graduate students and young professionals, purchased several of the units. A handful of parents bought units for their children who are undergraduate students at Vanderbilt. Other buyers included empty nesters working within walking distance of the project and people looking to trade in large suburban homes for urban convenience. A couple of buyers bought units as second-home pieds-à-terre in the city.

The initial absorption of the project was dramatic, recording 14 sales in one week. This market acceptance continued, and the project was entirely sold out months before completion—at a pace of 1.5 units per month, with sales exceeding expectations by $1 million. The return on investment is forecast to exceed projections by 30 percent. M2H Group views those results as a windfall from the intense management of the design process, careful supervision of construction costs, and shrewd pricing of units with close adherence to market demand from start to finish.

The ongoing management of the property will be overseen by the unit owners association (UOA) established for the property with help and guidance from a professional management company. The UOA's rules and restrictions are designed to protect the property value and maximize the residents' shared enjoyment of the property.

Experience Gained

Exceeding the M2H Group's expectations, 807 Eighteenth taught the developer several key lessons.

» Creative architectural design distinguished 807 Eighteenth from standard mid-rise condominium buildings. The strengths of the overall plan begin with the unique and intimate feel of the project compared to a standard mid-rise design. The courtyard and rowhouse street frontage are comforting and inviting rather than cold and intimidating. Floor plans that are unique to the project, and therefore to the marketplace, provide a level of individuality to the residences, adding to the success of the concept.

» Site constraints and the construction process are difficult to manage on an infill site. As in any urban setting, the site design has very little room to spare, making the project subject to a slower schedule at times and creating some frustrations for the contractors on the job.

» Combining concrete, steel, and stick frame was challenging. The combination of significant concrete, steel, and wood frame can be difficult and needs to be closely watched and managed by both the general contractor and the owner to ensure success.

Project Data: 807 Eighteenth

www.807eighteenth.com

Land Use Information

Site area: 22,500 square feet

Total dwelling units planned: 44

Total dwelling units completed: 46

Gross density: 92 units per acre

Average net density: 92 units per acre

Land Use Plan

	Acres	Percentage of Site
Attached residential	0.5	100

Development Cost Information

Site acquisition costs	$ 848,900
Site improvement costs	775,000
Construction costs	6,000,000
Soft costs	900,000
Total development cost	**$ 8,523,900**

Development Schedule

Planning started:	May 2003
Site purchased:	July 2004
Construction started:	July 2004
Sales started:	April 2004
First closing:	October 2005
Project completed:	January 2006

Project Team

Developer

M2H Group

Nashville, Tennessee

www.m2hgroup.com

General Contractor

Solomon Builders

Nashville, Tennessee

www.solomonbuilders.com

Site Planner

Civil Site Design Group

Nashville, Tennessee

Architect

EOA-Architects

Nashville, Tennessee

www.eoa-architects.com

Residential Unit Information

Unit Type (Bedroom/Bath)	Unit Size (Square Feet)	Number of Units Planned/Built	Range of Sales Prices
2/2.5 stacked townhome	1,392	8/8	$269,000–319,500
2/2.5 stacked townhome	1,410	0/4*	$319,000–350,400
2/2 flat	283	6/6	$277,900–305,000
1/1 flat	868	6/6	$169,900–190,500
1/1 flat	853	8/8	$185,700–210,800
1/1 flat	736	12/12	$150,725–185,300
3/2.5 stacked townhome	1,434	2/0*	$395,000

*The original three-bedroom units were three stories with half of the floor plate on the fourth floor (rooftop deck). When the two three-bedroom units were divided into four two-bedroom units, the developer gained square footage by using four full floors.

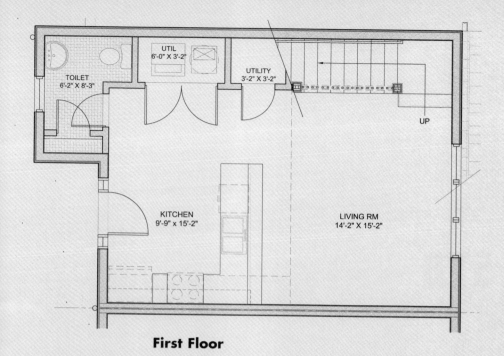

First Floor

TOILET
6'-2" X 8'-3"

UTIL
6'-0" X 3'-2"

UTILITY
3'-2" X 3'-2"

UP

KITCHEN
9'-9" x 15'-2"

LIVING RM
14'-2" X 15'-2"

One-bedroom, 1.5-bathroom sky loft floor plan. M2H Group

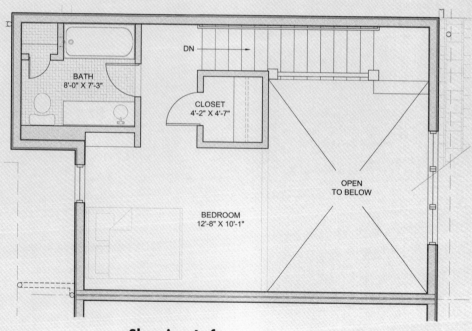

Sleeping Loft

DN

BATH
8'-0" X 7'-3"

CLOSET
4'-2" X 4'-7"

OPEN
TO BELOW

BEDROOM
12'-8" X 10'-1"

1400 ON 5TH

New York, New York

The revitalization of New York's Harlem was sparked by community activism and renewed interest among developers, nonprofit organizations, and government at all levels, eager to create public/private partnerships that have provided the tools—and the magnet—for residential projects.

1400 on 5th is an energy-efficient, nine-story, mixed-use building of nearly 200,000 square feet that includes 128 residential units, 30,782 square feet of ground-level retail space, and nine residential townhouses. Located between 115th and 116th streets in central Harlem, the building is New York City's first and only green residential development with an affordable component. Project partners are Full Spectrum New York, a 100-person, African American–owned, Harlem-based real estate development firm that conceptualized the project in 1996, and HRH Construction, a general contractor. Unlike during Harlem's earlier years, when architecture and interior design were dictated by white outsiders, now the local community of black architects, planners, and developers is taking part.

The building features such technological innovations as a geothermal system for heating and cooling, and 80 percent of the building was constructed with recycled building materials. Indoor air quality is superior, helped by use of paints, adhesives, carpets, and carpet padding with low volatile organic compound (VOC) content. The developers used bamboo flooring and Energy Star appliances and lighting fixtures, installed submetering, employed low-E (low-emittance) glass, and used gravel in the parking spaces to provide a pervious surface.

The Site

A subdivision of New York City located at the northern end of Manhattan and bordering on the Harlem and East rivers, Harlem is informally divided into three areas. Central and west Harlem begin at about 110th Street at Central Park North and extend to 155th Street, bounded on the west by the Hudson River and on the east by Fifth Avenue. East Harlem, also known as Spanish Harlem or El Barrio, runs from First Avenue to Fifth Avenue, and East 96th to East 125th streets. Its southern end straddles the imaginary line that divides white New York from black.

In what is known as the Gateway Area to Harlem, 1400 on 5th is located in the Harlem Empowerment Zone in an area considered south central Harlem. At the turn of the 20th century, five five-story apartment buildings occupied the site, and over the years, other residential development and retail stores were added. By the 1960s, most of the buildings had been demolished, leaving only an auto junkyard when plans for 1400 on 5th emerged. By the time Full Spectrum stepped in, the New York City–owned site was an urban brownfield requiring

environmental mitigation to reclaim the parcel. The land is zoned R7–2, which is a general residential district permitting both residential and commercial facilities.

One of the factors contributing to the selection of the site was transportation accessibility, which paralleled Full Spectrum's environmental philosophy. Located on Fifth Avenue, which is a main thoroughfare, the site is convenient to bus routes (M1, M2, M3, and M5 at Fifth and Madison avenues), subway (number 6 line at 116th and Lexington Avenue) transportation, and Metro-Rail commuter rail, and it is about ten minutes by car or taxi from LaGuardia Airport. It is ten blocks from the revitalized 125th Street commercial district.

History and Development

New York City's Harlem section is an incubator and a percolator of economic, social, and cultural change. The nation's largest African American community, Harlem did not start out that way. In the 18th and 19th centuries, successful Protestant, Roman Catholic, and later, prominent Jewish immigrants built magnificent homes in Harlem. When the "el" (elevated rail) was built, the population grew in both size and diversity. Three- and four-story brownstones and apartment buildings became the typical architecture.

1400 on 5th, in central Harlem, was designed to address sustainability from environmental, economic, and cultural perspectives. The condominium building is the first affordable urban mid-rise to qualify for the New York State Green Building Tax Credit, providing each homeowner with an average tax credit of $24,000 over a five-year period. Full Spectrum Building and Development

Poverty, crime, and urban blight characterized the area for years. World War I and an abundance of vacant properties attracted an influx of African Americans to Harlem; a new elite emerged, as well as a large working class that labored for white shopkeepers. Harlem teemed with creativity, and black writers, artists, and musicians established Harlem's jazz culture. The Harlem Renaissance began.

Today a second renaissance is occurring. New residential, commercial, and retail development is driving the change, bringing with it upwardly mobile black, white, and Hispanic middle-income homeowners and renters. Today's pioneers include young professionals whose families may have abandoned Harlem years ago. They are moving back to the old neighborhood because of Harlem's rich history and the relative affordability of condominiums, fixer-upper brownstone houses, and apartments that would cost substantially more in lower Manhattan.

In the current wave of urban renewal, vacant lots, abandoned brownstones and multifamily buildings, and empty commercial spaces are being developed to reclaim land and structures once frequented by drug dealers, thieves, and hookers. Most of the recent housing development has been limited-

Full Spectrum created a healthy living environment by using materials such as paints, adhesives, and carpets with low VOC content; bamboo flooring; and specialized filtration and mechanical systems to maximize fresh air and remove allergens.

Full Spectrum Building and Development

equity cooperatives, but condominiums are becoming a popular housing alternative. It is a big change from about two decades ago when substantial housing stock was taken by the city by foreclosure for nonpayment of taxes, and housing stock sank further into disrepair.

Developers are drawn to Harlem by federal funding programs and tax credits available to battered urban areas to compensate for a dearth of private sector lending, as well as 1992 legislation that matched city and state funds with about $300 million in investment capital. "At the time," explains Carlton Brown, chief operating officer of Full Spectrum New York, "the perception of crime was far greater than the reality, which is that the area had more vacant city land than most parts of the city, and the adjacent public housing had problems, but wasn't the prototypical housing project. Additionally, local Harlemites believe the presence of an Islamic mosque at 115th Street kept the 115th Street corridor relatively safe."

Over time, through stepped-up enforcement initiatives, the crime rate has fallen dramatically throughout the city and in Harlem as well, Brown said. "What has fallen more precipitously is the perception of crime. People feel like it is a safe place now." Amid this change is 1400 on 5th.

The site was owned by the city of New York. It is located across a 60-foot-wide street from 18,000 public housing units that run from Second to Seventh avenues and from 112th to 115th streets, an unlikely place for housing that would create value for middle-income buyers. It is one of thousands of properties sold since the 1990s by the city, which offered tax incentives, such as low-income housing tax credits, and programs that encouraged Full Spectrum and others to invest in Harlem's revitalization. In exchange for incentives, Full Spectrum agreed to sell a portion of units to residents earning between 80 and 165 percent of the area median income, providing between $60,000 and $120,000 in subsidies, depending on the size of the unit.

As the project labored through its formative stage, the Harlem real estate market had heated up. When former president Bill Clinton opened an office in Harlem ten blocks from 1400 on 5th, it added to the area's respectability. Nearby 125th Street, for years a major commercial corridor, had been revitalized by development of major retail chains, such as Starbucks, Old Navy, and Sprint. By the time 1400 moved closer to fruition, the market was ready for upscale condominium housing that targeted urban, and particularly African American, professionals who may have otherwise snubbed Harlem because of its earlier ghetto image.

Full Spectrum built a 195,569-square-foot, energy-efficient, nine-story, mixed-use building that includes 128 residential units on the second to ninth floors atop 30,782 square feet of ground-level retail space. Of the units, 43 are market rate; initial sales prices ranged from $185,000 to $600,000. The remaining 85 units were reserved for buyers with annual incomes between $50,000 and $104,000 (no more than 165 percent of the area media income), the segment of the population that has been frozen out of the Manhattan housing market. The building is predominantly two- and three-bedroom units designed to meet the need for larger units for families. Thirty-nine parking spaces are scheduled to be made available for purchase on an adjacent property.

The company's preliminary research revealed that potential buyers wanted more amenities, including updated technologies that are commonly found in affluent communities of New York City. Whereas a business center was once a popular amenity in a market-rate building, broadband Internet access is essential to today's buyers. Full Spectrum introduced broadband to this area of Harlem, despite the perception that no market for it would exist in a predominantly lower-income community. Buyers also wanted such market-rate amenities as granite countertops, wood floors, and a concierge. Full Spectrum met market demand. Buyers also wanted easy access to restaurants, a dry cleaner, and a health club, which Full Spectrum provided in the first-floor retail space.

Full Spectrum's philosophy is that the redevelopment of emerging urban communities must do more than offer shelter and that investment in housing in underserved communities must contribute to economic, social, and environmental sustainability and promote the well-being of all who live there.

"Everyone deserves affordable housing that is built in a way that sustains the environment," says Brown, whose company's objectives are founded on the notion of sustainable development. He believes that conventional construction practices produce more materials bound for the landfill and are costlier, too. So he incorporated recycled or renewable and highly energy-efficient materials: well-insulated, tightly sealed windows allow for a smaller heating and cooling system; factory-made prefabricated walls are cheaper than those built on site; lightweight composite recycled steel frame allows for less masonry.

Brown also believes in providing the tools that are necessary to empower residents. "Housing should provide infrastructure that is energy efficient, provide superior air quality, use renewable resources, and provide the necessary digital infrastructure to empower residents by bridging the digital divide. It should offer an architectural design that is culturally relevant to the prevailing culture of the community," he said.

Brown has a hierarchical approach to green building. Environmental impact occurs at three levels: micro, macro, and global. Microenvironment affects the people who live or work in the building; macro affects the community where the development is located; global affects the world. Brown believes focusing on microenvironmental issues has a residual effect on the greater community.

Financing

Full Spectrum needed four years to find financiers willing to take the risk and support an affordable, environmentally sustainable, and technologically smart building for what was generally considered an emerging urban market. Doubters questioned Full Spectrum's ability to assemble a financing package and then attract professionals who would want to buy into Harlem's revival. Bankers encouraged Brown to build all subsidized housing for lower-income households because they knew a market existed for it, whereas upscale housing was chancy.

Momentum to build began when Full Spectrum established its credentials and financial capability with the New York City Department of Housing Preservation and Development (HPD) and the New York City Housing Partnership, which eventually led to the requisite building and environmental approvals being obtained. Full Spectrum's partners then secured construction financing from Fleet Bank.

Full Spectrum also pursued nontraditional funding sources. The project became the first urban mid-rise with an affordable component to qualify for the New York State Green Building Tax Credit, providing each homeowner with an estimated average tax credit of $22,250 over five years. The tax credit, unveiled in 2000, was the first of its kind in the nation and has allowed a developer of environmentally friendly buildings to write off as much as $6 million on its tax bill.

Before closing on the construction loan, Housing Development Fund Company (HDFC), Inc., and Full Spectrum entered into a site development agreement in which Full Spectrum would construct the project, acquire title to the commercial units, and sell the residential units. Under the agreement, HDFC agreed to monitor performance under the approved development schedule and to be the liaison with HPD, keeping the agency informed of development progress. In 2002, HRH Construction was named general contractor—forming 1400 on 5th Development LLC. The limited liability company consists of Full Spectrum Building 116th Street Development LLC and HRH Construction LLC. Full Spectrum is the managing member and has majority ownership of the LLC.

Construction of the residential and retail portions was financed with $40 million through a mix of public and private funding:

» Fleet National Bank, Fleet Real Estate Finance Group, provided a $25 million construction loan, with additional funding from Fannie Mae.

» Full Spectrum contributed equity of $3.3 million (residential) and $249,000 (retail).

» New York City Housing Development Corporation provided a public subsidy of $1.9 million for the income-restricted units. HPD provided the land, initiated a rezoning, and provided a subsidy of $3.8 million.

» Bank of America provided $27.2 million (in construction and mezzanine financing, together with Fannie Mae).

» The U.S. Department of Housing and Urban Development provided a Section 108 loan of $3.5 million for financing the construction of the commercial space.

» The Alliance for Neighborhood Commerce Home Ownership Revitalization (ANCHOR), administered jointly by the New York City Housing Partnership and HPD, coordinated public subsidy and private investment and was primarily responsible for design and implementation.

» Harlem Community Development Corporation, a subsidiary of the Empire State Development Corporation, provided financing of $890,000 for the retail portion through the Metropolitan Economic Revitalization Fund for a permanent mortgage for the retail space.

» New York State Energy Research and Development Authority provided more than $500,000 in grants for research, design, and incorporation of green building and energy conservation features into the building.

The project was one of five that received a total of $18.8 million in tax breaks under New York State's Green Building Tax Credit program, which was the nation's first tax-incentive program for the design, construction, or rehabilitation of environmentally friendly buildings. The tax credit to Full Spectrum was $1.77 million. The project was also part of HPD's ANCHOR program, designed to spur economic development through colocated retail opportunities and housing in distressed areas. Commercial tenants eventually included Ginger Restaurant, Harlem World Sports Club, Grisula's on Fifth Dry Cleaners, and Carver Bank.

Planning, Design, and Construction

High-tech and environmentally friendly features make 1400 on 5th unusual in its market, as does the range in unit size, from a 900-square-foot one-bedroom unit to 3,900-square-foot four-bedroom triplexes. Most units have at least two bathrooms, and most have home office areas. Among the amenities are a 24-hour concierge, valet cleaning and laundry services, a business center, landscaped private gardens, a package room for pickups and delivery, a one-year health club membership, and parking.

The mixed-use building contains nine stories, with 120 residential units on the second to ninth floors and attached townhouse-style units. Six ground-floor spaces house commercial tenants. Space for 39 outdoor parking units is adjacent to the building.

All units are connected to a broadband network that uses phased-array antennae technology to provide up to three megabytes per second at less than the cost of dial-up service. A smart laundry (located on each floor) and smart security system give residents remote access from their units to laundry

Smart technologies provide residents with conveniences such as broadband and wireless Internet, and a buildingwide security system. Full Spectrum Building and Development

center controls, security cameras, and building access control. The buildingwide digital network connects each unit to the concierge, the building superintendent, and retail tenant service providers; the business center on site includes three conference rooms equipped with Mac and PC workstations, video conferencing, printers, copiers, and entertainment and distance-learning facilities. The building also has wireless connectivity in all outdoor space.

1400 on 5th was designed to reflect the West African heritage—which architect Roberta Washington, the building's designer, says is defined by warm earth tones, open space, and concern for the land—and conveys traditional West African values. The architecture is complemented by African-influenced symbols throughout the building. Mframa-dan Adinkra, the West African Adinkra symbol that suggests a well-built home is one that can withstand unfavorable weather conditions, is depicted throughout the facility. The building wraps around an interior courtyard landscaped with native trees and shrubs.

The structure's design is an example of contemporary, culturally specific urban architecture that addresses environmental sustainability. To achieve harmony with the environment, the building features geothermal heating and cooling, condensing hot water heaters, a high-performance air filtration system, and recycled and renewable building materials. All appliances and lighting fixtures carry the Energy Star label. All materials used in construction have a high recycled content or were manufactured from rapidly renewable resources: steel framing, reinforced slag concrete, bamboo floors, and gypsum wallboard. In 1997, Full Spectrum budgeted the construction cost at $135 per square foot. In 2002, the actual cost was $142.

The project marked several green building "firsts": for energy design, it received a New Construction Whole Building Award from the New York State Energy Research and Development Authority as the first green urban affordable housing development; it qualified for a U.S. Green Building Council Leadership in Energy and Environmental Design (LEED) Award. The building meets the state's green building criteria because it was constructed with 70 percent recycled and renewable resources and uses 36.5 percent less energy than is permissible by the New York State Energy Code because of a high-performance building envelope (doors, roof, walls, foundation, insulation, seals, windows, and thermal shell) and a geothermal system.

Using geothermal energy for heating and air conditioning—a method that takes advantage of the relatively unchanging underground temperature of the earth, which is

The project features artwork that reflects the West African heritage. Full Spectrum Building and Development

cooler than the air in summer and warmer in winter—the building reduces reliance on fossil fuels. In a geothermal system, water travels within a closed-loop pipe system. During the winter, the water warms as it travels through below-ground pipes and then distributes the heat to each unit. In the summer, the process is reversed, drawing heat from the unit instead of injecting cold air into it. Replacing both a furnace and an air-conditioning system, the geothermal system is considered the most energy-efficient heating and cooling system available, averting the production of 700 tons of greenhouse gas annually, thereby helping reduce global warming. The system is environmentally friendly; studies show that about 70 percent of the energy used in a geothermal system is renewable energy from the ground, and the remainder is clean, electrical energy that is used to concentrate heat and transport it.

The mechanical system exhausts all bathrooms and kitchens and delivers fresh filtered air to the public corridors and each unit. The mechanical system removes allergens from the air, thereby eliminating the environmental triggers for allergy and asthma attacks that are said to be the highest in the nation in Harlem.

Steel construction was chosen because of poor soil conditions, a height limit, and a tight budget, which made it a better option than poured concrete, which is the norm in residential construction in New York City. The choice resulted in a lighter building and avoided cold-weather construction delays typically caused by the time and conditions required for concrete to cure. It also enabled the use of an exterior panel system that attached to the steel superstructure, which resulted in cost savings in both material and labor.

Steel construction also helped secure U.S. Green Building Council LEED certification, a voluntary national standard for developing high-performance, sustainable buildings that brings with it a variety of cost and other benefits. The steel used at 1400 on 5th was up to 70 to 80 percent recycled.

Marketing, Management, Tenants, and Performance

Although Harlem has grown increasingly diverse in recent years, the concept of mixing market-rate with affordable condominium apartments and townhouses marked uncharted marketing territory. Occupancy began in June 2003, and by late 2005, although 95 percent of the apartment units were sold, only three of the nine townhouse condominiums were sold.

1400 on 5th was the second condominium project in Harlem. The other relatively new type of for-sale multifamily housing was the limited-equity co-op in which the unit occupant is considered a tenant who holds a long-term lease and owns

stock. The closest comparable condominium offered three-bedroom, 930-square-foot units, but 1400 offered 1,200-square-foot units, a size usually available in brownstones that cost as much as $900,000 at the time, and not in apartment units. In June 2002, when the groundbreaking ceremonies were held, comparable housing cost between nearly $500,000 and $1.5 million.

To test the salability of units, focus groups of bankers, engineers, teachers, and other college-educated professionals were assembled to learn whether middle-income buyers would live in Harlem. The research targeted young African Americans, Latinos, and others who had an affinity for Harlem because a family member had lived there or because of its cultural heritage. Research found that people in this target market would live in Harlem, but they had caveats: public safety, services and amenities, and unit size. Full Spectrum eventually received more than 5,000 requests for applications.

Affordable units were sold through a lottery held by HPD, and applications were available on Full Spectrum's Web site. Applicants were required to have good credit and purchase a unit for owner occupancy only. Of the 128 units, 85 were available to households with incomes between $52,000 and $103,000; these income-restricted homes were priced from $158,000 to $272,000. The remaining units were available to households with incomes over $89,000 and were priced from $127,000 to $700,000. Mortgages could be obtained with as little as 5 percent down, and closing cost rebates, real estate tax abatements, and Green Building Tax Credits were available to qualified purchasers.

The initial sales price of the townhouses was $650,000; by late 2005, the sales price had jumped to $1.3 million. The subsidized apartment units were sold at $175 to $200 per square foot, and the market-rate units at $600 per square foot.

For the market-rate units, Full Spectrum hired 15-year-old Harlem-based Griffin Real Estate Group, Inc., because of its familiarity with Harlem real estate. Griffin joint ventured with Marketing Directors, whose specialty was marketing luxury housing.

Marketing the condominiums had to follow an HPD guideline requiring outreach to the local community. To do that, Griffin held weekly informational meetings at four or five area churches with large congregations, such as Abyssinian Baptist Church and Mount Moriah Church, which are important institutions within the local African American community. Griffin also marketed the units to employees at Mount Sinai, Harlem, North General, and St. Luke's hospitals and Columbia University, all located within the catchment areas of Community

Full Spectrum's preliminary research revealed that, in addition to wanting more amenities, potential buyers wanted easy access to neighborhood shops and services. 1400 on 5th's 30,782 square feet of ground-level retail is filled by restaurants, a dry cleaner, and a health club. Full Spectrum Building and Development

DEVELOPING CONDOMINIUMS

Boards 10 and 11—advisory boards appointed by borough presidents to deal with land use, zoning, and other community matters—both of which the Fifth Avenue property straddles. HPD required that 50 percent of the units be sold to purchasers living within the areas covered by those two community boards, said Carole Griffin. Her group held "cultivation events" targeting a broad income range of members of fraternities and sororities and socially based organizations that were invited to preview the units.

Griffin used traditional advertising outlets for million-dollar properties to market the market-rate units. It contacted all the brokerage firms that show properties in Harlem, advertised in the *New York Times* print and online outlets, and used the Real Estate Board of New York's Multiple Listing Service.

Experience Gained

"1400 was the first project we did to address sustainability from environmental, economic, and cultural perspectives, and it eventually served as a model for a larger project [12 stories] adjacent, called the Kalahari," Brown said. "We took the lessons we learned in how we can reinvest in an urban community without increasing capital costs."

» **Enforce green building compliance with contractors.** Full Spectrum learned that standard contractors were unfamiliar with environmentally friendly construction, more accustomed to work habits and materials that they had used for decades, and were either unwilling or reluctant to change. This situation created even more work for subcontractors. "We learned that tradespeople had no particular regard for their own health or safety, and less concern for the health and safety of the people who were going to live in the building," Brown said. In some cases, in spite of promises to comply with green requirements, actual work failed to comply, forcing Full Spectrum to police contractors and have work redone. "At the time, professional organizations promoted green development through training programs and other educational activities, but knowledge did not filter through to the workers," Brown said. Full Spectrum subsequently enforced casualty clauses in its contracts that required green building compliance and imposed noncompliance penalties.

» **Seek buy-in.** Full Spectrum found it challenging to introduce Harlem to a new product, incorporating green building and new construction techniques and tapping an emerging market. Private funders, government officials, and community members were initially skeptical that an environmentally friendly mixed-use and mixed-income building would be an economic asset to Harlem. To secure buy-in from those constituencies, Full Spectrum learned the value of participating in many meetings and presentations targeting specific audiences. It also learned that the company benefited from including experts in the presentations to educate and provide specific technical information that was beyond the expertise of the company's team.

» **Propose solutions.** Full Spectrum learned that by providing a range of solutions to stakeholders it ensured the solution was acceptable from the developer's perspective while also enabling stakeholders to provide input and brainstorm "outside the box" alternatives falling within the realm of feasible solutions.

» **Establish credibility.** Full Spectrum found that the key to stakeholder buy-in was establishing credibility. One approach it found valuable was serving as environmental technical coordinator for the highly acclaimed Solaire, a luxury, green building project in lower Manhattan's Battery Park area developed by the Albanese Development Corporation.

Project Data: 1400 on 5th

www.1400on5th.com

Land Use Information

Site area: 54,915 square feet

Total dwelling units: 129

Land Use Plan

	Zoning area
Commercial	14,528 square feet
Residential	175,266 square feet
Parking	39 spaces

Residential Unit Information

Type of Apartments (Bedroom)	Income-Restricted Units	Unrestricted Units	Unit Size (Square Feet)	Minimum Sale Prices
1	6	1	891	$160,000
2	74	16	946	$175,000
3	5	26	1,453	$235,000
Townhouses	0	9	3,851	$900,000
Total	**85**	**52**		

Development Cost Information

Site acquisition cost	$ 1.1 million
Construction cost:	
Retail	3.3 million
Residential and parking	28.0 million
Soft costs	21.0 million
Total cost	**$53.4 million**

Development Schedule

Planning started:	Fall 1997
Construction started:	August 2002
Sales started	
Lottery, subsidized units:	December 2002
Market rate:	Summer 2003
First closing:	August 2004
Project completed:	August 2005

Project Team

Developers

Full Spectrum NY
New York, New York
www.fullspectrumny.com

HRH Construction
New York, New York
www.hrhconstruction.com

Architects

Roberta Washington
Architects, PC
New York, New York
www.robertawashington.com

William Q. Brothers III
Architects
New York, New York

Structural Engineer

Trevor Salmon Consulting
Engineers, PC
New York, New York

MEP Engineer

P.A. Collins P.E.
New York, New York
www.pacollinspe.com

Civil Engineer

Mike Pein P.E.
Bellmore, New York

Geothermal Well Design

Water Energy Distributions, Inc.
Atkinson, New Hampshire

Landscape Architect

EKLA
Brooklyn, New York
www.eklastudio.com

Building Systems Consultants

Steven Winter Associates
Norwalk, Connecticut
www.swinter.com

Sales

Griffin Group
New York, New York

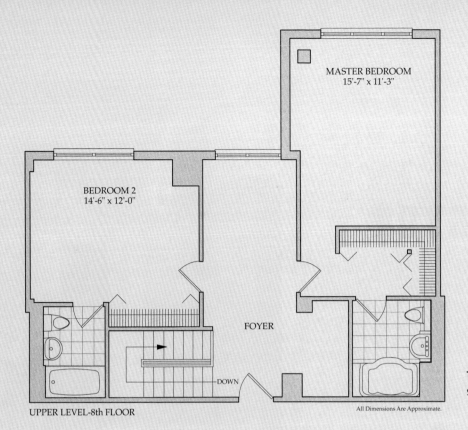

MASTER BEDROOM
15'-7" x 11'-3"

BEDROOM 2
14'-6" x 12'-0"

FOYER

DOWN

UPPER LEVEL-8th FLOOR

All Dimensions Are Approximate.

Three-bedroom floor plan. Full
Spectrum Building and Development

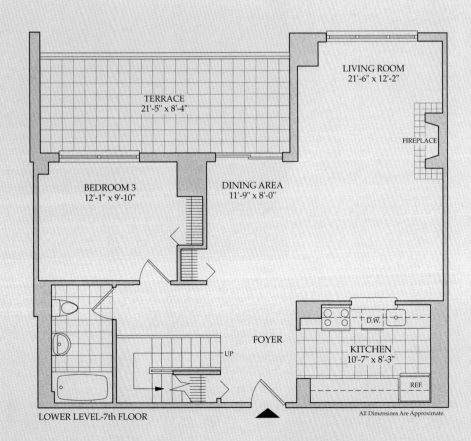

LIVING ROOM
21'-6" x 12'-2"

TERRACE
21'-5" x 8'-4"

FIREPLACE

BEDROOM 3
12'-1" x 9'-10"

DINING AREA
11'-9" x 8'-0"

D.W.

FOYER

UP

KITCHEN
10'-7" x 8'-3"

REF.

LOWER LEVEL-7th FLOOR

All Dimensions Are Approximate.

KENSINGTON PARK

Richfield, Minnesota

Kensington Park is a mixed-use infill project that features 96 flats and 14 townhomes, all under condominium ownership, and 27,000 square feet of ground-floor retail space. The flats are located in two four-story buildings, one of which has ground-floor retail space facing busy Lyndale Avenue. The townhomes are located along the portion of the site that faces an adjacent residential street, and two additional free-standing retail buildings also face Lyndale Avenue.

Kensington Park is the third phase of the Lyndale Gateway redevelopment in the city of Richfield, a first-tier suburb south of Minneapolis. The first two phases include the reconstruction of Lyndale Avenue and a combination of apartments for seniors, offices, and townhomes located across Lyndale Avenue from the Kensington Park site.

Kensington Park's three-acre site was once a magnet for crime and drug activity but is now a safe, mixed-use, pedestrian-friendly community. Sam Newberg

The condominiums were priced from $139,200 to $292,900, and the townhomes from $303,000 to $329,500. The target market consisted of empty nesters from the immediate area and young professionals drawn to the area for proximity to employment.

The Site

The Cornerstone Group was immediately attracted to the Kensington Park site because of its interest in infill development and the mixed-use opportunity for both retail and housing construction. The site itself previously contained 18 retail businesses along Lyndale and seven single-family homes along Aldrich. The area immediately surrounding the site includes a variety of uses, including an assortment of freestanding retail and multifamily rental apartments to the north along Lyndale Avenue. Single-family homes exist to the west of the site, as well as to the east of the Lyndale Gateway redevelopment area. To the south, across Lyndale Avenue and 77th Street, are a Hampton Inn and a retail power center that includes tenants such as Best Buy and Borders.

Site plan. Elness Swenson Graham Architects

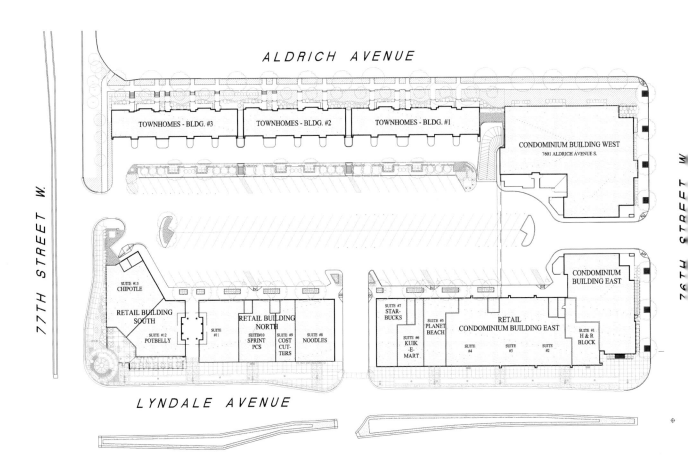

Kensington Park occupies one city block, about three acres within the Lyndale Gateway. Lyndale Avenue is on the east of the project, 77th Street runs along the southern border, Aldrich Avenue is on the west, and 76th Street is to the north. Lyndale Avenue is a busy four-lane street that runs north-south through the city and connects to the interchange with Interstate 494 one block south of the site. Also four-lane streets, 76th and 77th run east to west (77th Street is busier and includes a center island). They meet one-half mile west of the site at the interchange with Interstate 35 West.

In addition to proximity to the Interstate 494/35W interchange, Kensington Park has good access to significant employment sources. Minneapolis–St. Paul International Airport and Mall of America are located approximately three miles to the east along I-494, and a large amount of employment is located along and near the I-494 corridor to the west, including the Best Buy headquarters, which is one mile away. Also, downtown Minneapolis is located just nine miles to the north along I-35W. This proximity to employment and the airport were primary reasons buyers chose to purchase units at Kensington Park.

Development Process

Kensington Park was developed by the Cornerstone Group, a woman-owned real estate development company that was formed in 1993. The small Twin Cities–based company employs 12 staff members, focused on housing development and creating vibrant neighborhoods. To date, the Cornerstone Group has completed $150 million worth of urban housing projects, and every community in which the company builds receives a donation from the developer to support environmental, educational, social, or arts programs.

The city of Richfield has been seeking to redevelop key commercial sections of the city, dubbed "gateways," since the 1980s. Kensington Park is the third phase of the Lyndale Gateway redevelopment projects. The first two phases involved reconstructing Lyndale Avenue and creating Main Street Village, including 40 townhomes, 161 apartments for seniors, and 38,000 square feet of office space. Other successful projects in the city include the 5,000-employee Best Buy headquarters campus, which opened in 2004 at the Penn Gateway, the intersection of Penn Avenue and Interstate 494.

Richfield is a post–World War II suburb, and original development in the neighborhood consists of one- and one-and-a-half-story homes, with one-story commercial uses along major corridors such as Lyndale Avenue. Most of the single-family homes in the area remain, whereas a large number of the original commercial uses have been redeveloped over the years.

By the 1980s, many of the area retail uses, including those on the site, were blighted, and the street was attracting crime and drug activity. This deterioration was a concern for area residents and city officials, who targeted the Lyndale Gateway area for redevelopment. Several proposals for projects on the site were submitted by developers and considered by the city between the mid-1980s and 2000, but none were dense enough to make economic sense. Thus, in 2000, the city issued a request for proposals (RFP) for the site. The Cornerstone Group was one of three developers to submit a proposal, and its proposal was accepted.

The site was originally zoned B-2, which allowed for the existing one-story businesses that fronted Lyndale Avenue and single-family residential along Aldrich Avenue, but the city of Richfield rezoned the entire site as a planned unit development (PUD) by the time the RFP was issued. With the PUD zoning, no specific density requirement applied, but area residents and the city made it clear that a height restriction of four stories existed for the project.

A complicated and at times problematic issue was site assembly, which involved the acquisition of seven single-family homes and 11 commercial parcels occupied by the 18 businesses. The city preferred that the Cornerstone Group acquire the properties, although the city assisted with negotiating purchase prices and relocation costs. Most property owners were willing sellers, having been aware of redevelopment plans for years. Purchase agreements were privately brokered for all properties except two businesses, which were ultimately condemned by the city.

In addition to the retail and residential property acquisition, the developer also had to acquire small pieces and slivers of public right-of-way, including sections of land along streets, as well as a public alley. Those parcels had to be deeded to the Cornerstone Group, which involved replatting and creating a Registered Land Survey (RLS), a three-dimensional survey in lieu of a traditional Common Interest Community Plat required for condominiums and planned communities in Minnesota.

The Cornerstone Group chose to develop condominiums on the site primarily because high-density housing was required to make the project work financially. Market research indicated demand for retail and condominiums, because the office and apartment markets were soft at the time. Thus, the Cornerstone Group decided to do a mixed-use project. Overall, the project worked because of the appropriate mix of uses, high density, a generally healthy condominium market, and city investment.

A combination of building materials and design elements blends the townhomes and condominium buildings of Kensington Park with the original development in the surrounding post–World War II suburban neighborhood.

Sam Newberg

Planning, Design, and Construction

The site plan consists of four parts: a west condominium building, an east condominium building with ground-floor retail, a row of 14 townhomes, and two freestanding retail buildings. All four parts are arranged in a horseshoe around an interior surface parking lot intended primarily for retail customers. Underground parking is provided for condominium residents, and the townhomes have tuck-under garage parking for two cars in the lower level at the back of the units. The townhouse garages are accessed from the guest parking lot.

The two condominium buildings are located at the north end of the site, along 76th Street. The east condominium building's retail space faces Lyndale Avenue, and the west condominium building faces Aldrich Avenue. The townhomes face Aldrich Avenue and act as a buffer between the rest of the project and the single-family homes located across the street to the west. The freestanding retail buildings are located along Lyndale Avenue on the southern end of the site, nearest 77th Street, which maximizes exposure to the traffic for the retail tenants. The city of Richfield required three automobile entrances to the project, one each on 76th and 77th streets and one on Lyndale Avenue. These entrances serve both the retail customers and residents.

The architect created a plan to integrate all of the uses on the site while still maintaining high-quality, individual design. Because each building faces not just a street but also a parking lot, care was taken to hide truck-loading areas for the commercial component, garage doors, and dumpsters as much as possible. To create a pedestrian-oriented environment, especially along Lyndale Avenue, Kensington Park has wide sidewalks with trees planted in a six-foot-wide strip between street curb and public sidewalk, and several retail tenants (three restaurants and a coffee shop) have outdoor seating along the sidewalk. The Richfield Housing and Redevelopment Authority (HRA) invested in the streetscape improvements to help create a gateway effect for the development. However, one drawback of the site design is the lack of on-street parking along Lyndale Avenue, which would have provided an additional buffer between the sidewalk and moving traffic on the street.

The other three streets surrounding the site also have public sidewalks. Trees are planted along 76th Street, but not 77th. A planting strip with mature trees remains along Aldrich Avenue, which enhances the curb appeal of the townhomes as well as provides shade.

The four-story condominium buildings roughly match the building height of Main Street Village across Lyndale Avenue to the east, giving the street cross section a sense of balance. They are significantly taller, however, than the one-story freestanding retail uses located to the north of 76th Street along Lyndale. Increasing land values will probably spur future redevelopment in this corridor to match the four-story building heights of the recent development.

The architect and developer spent time in design charrettes with city staff members and the sales team to establish design standards. As a result, they decided to use a combination of building materials, including brick, Hardipanel (a substitute for stucco that lasts longer, does not stain as easily, and is less prone to cracking), metal panels, and glass. Circular steel crowns adorn the building rooftops at the corners of Lyndale Avenue at 77th and 76th streets, and a steel tower rises between the retail buildings to add height and dimension.

Pedestrian entrances are numerous at Kensington Park. Every retail tenant has two entrances, one along Lyndale and one off the parking lot. Townhomes have pedestrian entrances located on stoops that face Aldrich Avenue. Each condominium building has pedestrian access from both the street and the parking lot.

Typical to mixed-use, infill projects, the tight site tested the creativity of the design and construction teams. Orienting the townhomes to face exterior streets meant their back doors faced the retail and surface parking in the center of the site. To create privacy and buffer this interaction, the townhomes were separated by grading, a retaining wall, a fence, and a line of newly planted trees.

The teams were further tested to ensure that both the condominium buildings and the freestanding retail building complied with the Americans with Disabilities Act. With entrances on both sides of the retail and condominium buildings, both sides had to be level.

Additionally, the project team gave special consideration to delivery truck circulation. The underground parking area, which is larger than the two footprints of the condominium buildings and is located below a portion of the surface parking lot, needed to be reinforced structurally to ensure delivery trucks could use that portion of the parking area.

The 96 condominium units range in size from 679-square-foot studios to 1,482-square-foot two-bedroom plus den units. The 14 townhomes are all 1,671 square feet. The unit mix of the condominiums is 17 percent studios, 31 percent one bedroom, 20 percent one bedroom plus den, 14 percent two bedroom, and 6 percent two bedroom plus den.

Each townhome unit contains tuck-under two-car garages. There are 117 underground parking spaces for the 96 condo-

minium units, a ratio of 1.2 spaces per unit, which is somewhat low for a suburban condominium development in the Twin Cities. However, there is exactly one space per bedroom (117 bedrooms in the two condominium buildings if the 19 studios are counted as containing a bedroom) in the project, which is a common rule of thumb used by condominium developers with regard to parking ratios.

Parking for retail is perhaps the biggest challenge of all, partly because of the current tenant mix, which includes three restaurants plus a coffee shop. There are 146 off-street parking spaces, which equates to 5.3 spaces per 1,000 square feet of retail area. The industry standard for restaurant uses is ten spaces per 1,000 square feet, and with so much of the space occupied by restaurants, a parking shortage often exists, especially at lunch time.

A small number of the 146 spaces are intended for guests of condominium residents. The parking shortage is exacerbated by the fact that some condominium residents occasionally park in the surface spaces, and employees—who are supposed to park off site—use the lot as well.

Because each building faces not just a street but also a parking lot, care was taken to hide truck loading areas for the commercial component, garage doors, and dumpsters as much as possible. Sam Newberg

Financing

Kensington Park was financed from a number of sources. The Richfield Housing and Redevelopment Authority provided the required 20 percent equity for the project, and M&I Bank provided a loan for the remaining 80 percent. Because the HRA provided 100 percent of the required equity, the city negotiated a deal to defer the $540,000 developer fee until the city began to see a return on its investment from the sales proceeds. The Cornerstone Group provided a $500,000 letter of credit.

M&I's loan required that 40 percent of the retail space be preleased and 50 percent of the units presold with 5 percent earnest money. The preleasing requirement for the retail space proved difficult, because construction was to take 18 months, and few tenants, besides national franchise restaurants, are willing to sign leases that far in advance. The developer did, however, find enough national franchises to lease over 40 percent of the retail space, allowing the project to move ahead.

The Richfield HRA created a 25-year tax increment financing (TIF) district for the site, which will be paid off through increased tax revenue over that time. The city also issued $6 million in general obligation bonds to help finance acquisition and relocation costs. Half would be paid back directly from sales proceeds as the units closed, and half would be paid back over the life of the TIF district. The district is expected to pay off in 11 years.

The developer received another $2.2 million from grants and other HRA funding sources to assist with the enormous site assembly cost. This funding included a Livable Communities Act demonstration grant ($500,000) from the Metropolitan Council (the Twin Cities' regional planning authority) for architectural enhancements and underground parking. The Minnesota Housing Finance Agency provided $300,000 in second mortgage assistance for approximately 20 units, or $10,000 to $15,000 per unit.

Marketing, Management, Tenants, and Performance

Predevelopment market studies for the condominium and townhome units indicated a vast majority of potential buyers would be empty nesters drawn from the vicinity. Kensington Park owners, however, have moved from all sections of the metropolitan area, attracted by the proximity of jobs in the I-494 corridor and downtown Minneapolis.

Approximately two-thirds of condominium buyers were younger couples and single professionals, and the remaining one-third are empty nesters, age 55 and older. Of the former category, most buyers were in their 30s and 40s, and the singles were overwhelmingly women. Approximately 10 percent of buyers were investors, especially among the smaller condominium units. Townhome buyers were split evenly between younger couples and empty nesters.

The condominium and townhome sales effort began in April 2003 with the use of an off-site sales trailer. Sales were very slow at first but steadily gained momentum, especially when the sales trailer moved on site in November 2003. At that point the project was half sold, and sales remained consistent through spring 2004. A significant amount of competitive product hit the market that spring, and Kensington Park sales dropped off precipitously. At that time, and during other stages of the sales effort, the Cornerstone Group and sales team offered free 42-inch flat-screen televisions, granite countertop upgrades, or monetary promotions to help with upgrades or closing costs. The first buyers moved into the townhomes in November 2004 and into the condominiums in January 2005.

Sales of condominium units at Kensington Park have been slower than anticipated. The Cornerstone Group originally projected that all units would be sold out within two years, but as of August 2006, after about three and a half years of sales, four of the 96 condominiums and one of the townhomes remain on the market. Sales rebounded in 2005, partly because much of the competition at that time was priced higher, but a wide-ranging housing slump has affected sales since then.

Sales were strongest for units priced under $200,000, which included studios and one bedrooms, and for the largest, most-expensive units, such as two bedroom plus dens and townhomes. One-bedroom plus den units and especially two-bedroom units in the $250,000 to $300,000 price range sold the slowest.

Several promotional events were held for Kensington Park, including a groundbreaking ceremony, open houses for Realtors, holiday parties, a grand opening party, and several promotional events with a local radio station. The Cornerstone Group also hired a public relations firm to help report and promote events. Several articles about the project appeared in local newspapers.

The developer anticipated a return on investment of between 12 percent and 14 percent. Because of carrying costs, that will likely be 10 to 12 percent when the project is eventually sold out. At the time of writing, the retail space is 70 percent leased, mostly by national franchises. The leasing agent reports substantial interest but cites high rents ($22 to $34 per square foot) as a reason that service-oriented businesses such as dry cleaners have found leasing a challenge at Kensington Park. As indicated previously, some potential tenants are deterred because parking is an issue at certain peak times of day.

Separate management entities handle the residential and retail portions of Kensington Park. All are contracted, and there is no on-site management or caretakers. The two management entities cooperate in shared-cost issues and on two reciprocal easement agreements—one for the shared site and parking lot, and the other for the east condominium building because it has three stories of residential over ground-floor retail space.

The townhomes, condominiums, and retail space have separate operating budgets, which makes accounting complicated. Additionally, shared budgets exist for the surface parking lot, grounds, and some utilities, as well as insurance costs for the shared building.

Only national franchise restaurants were willing to sign leases before construction; therefore, only a small portion of Kensington Park's retail space is occupied by locally owned shops. Sam Newberg

Market studies suggested that empty nesters would purchase many of the units at Kensington Park. Although some empty nesters did purchase units, more than two-thirds of the condominiums and townhomes attracted young couples and single professionals. Sam Newberg

Lyndale Gateway LLC, which is owned by the Cornerstone Group, owns the retail component and is sole member of the retail association. After 75 percent of the units were sold and closed, the homeowners association was turned over from Lyndale Gateway LLC to the residents. Therefore, Lyndale Gateway LLC does not own any portion of residential portion except unsold units.

The homeowners association is unusual because it is set up as a Registered Land Survey, which is different from traditional condominium ownership. With an RLS, each household owns its unit from "paint to paint," but the separating walls and common areas, including garage parking spaces, are all owned collectively by the association rather than as a prorated share per unit.

Rules and regulations govern all properties. A common issue that arises in mixed-use developments is providing quiet, peaceful enjoyment to the residents of their homes. For example, retailers and restaurants cannot blare loud music outside or have deliveries before or after certain hours.

As indicated earlier, shared parking also creates some enforcement issues for the management company. Residents are required to park underground, and only their guests can use the surface lot. With the shortage of parking that exists, each additional space taken by the wrong user affects the retailers, so parking is monitored closely.

Experience Gained

The Cornerstone Group learned many lessons from the development of Kensington Park, mostly related to the benefits and drawbacks of a mix of uses built on a small site.

» **Buyers are attracted to mixed-use development.** Kensington Park buyers appreciate having amenities such as restaurants and services on site and in a pedestrian-oriented environment, with tenants such as Starbucks being an especially strong selling point.

» **Maintaining midrange prices attracted buyers amid the 2005 condominium boom.** The average per square foot price for condominiums ($215 per square foot) was an attractive value for buyers in a market that has generally eclipsed that price in the past couple of years.

» **Infill sites need careful construction phasing.** The retail tenant spaces, particularly the three restaurants and Starbucks, were completed a few months ahead of the condominium buildings. Thus, as construction continued on the condominiums, construction vehicles tied up the shared parking lot, which conflicted with retail customers trying to find parking. The developer recommends opening all uses at the same time or completing the housing and infrastructure improvements ahead of the retail portions to avoid this situation.

» **Attractively design the rear side of buildings in projects with interior activity.** If the Cornerstone Group were to do the project again, it would have enhanced the rear of the townhomes with additional brickwork and visual interest because the property really has no back side.

» **The smallest units attracted investors but not homeowners.** The studio units, which range from 679 to 758 square feet, sold well, but primarily to investors who rent them out. Also, these smaller units do not necessarily have windows in the sleeping areas. In future projects, the Cornerstone Group is not planning to develop any units under 800 square feet because they do not seem to be attractive to homeowners.

» **Retail space should be flexible; otherwise it limits the type of tenants.** Kensington Park retail space was not planned for enough heating, ventilation, and air conditioning tonnage and electrical capacity because the project does not have enough 400-amp panels. This lack somewhat limits the type of tenants in the long term or requires substantial cost investments for tenant buildout.

» **Preleasing requirements for parking restricted retail tenants.** Parking was the largest issue, and the problem largely stems from the lender's requirement that 40 percent of the space be preleased before financing was approved. The only tenants willing to sign leases that far in advance were national restaurant chain outlets. As a result, the project has too many parking-intensive restaurants, resulting in a parking shortage. Consequently, prospective tenants cite the parking shortage as a drawback and look elsewhere for space. Had the lender's preleasing requirements not driven the leasing process, the developer posits one fewer restaurant lease would have been signed, which would require less parking and would have allowed additional services, such as dry cleaners and florists, to be attracted to the project.

Project Data: Kensington Park

www.kensingtonpark.info

Land Use Information

Site area: 3 acres

Total dwelling units: 110

Gross density: 36.67 units per acre

Total parking spaces: 117 spaces

Spaces per unit: 1.21

Retail/guest surface parking: 146 spaces

Parking ratio per 1,000 square feet of retail: 5.3

One-bedroom floor plan (below), and two-bedroom floor plan (facing page). Lyndale Gateway LLC

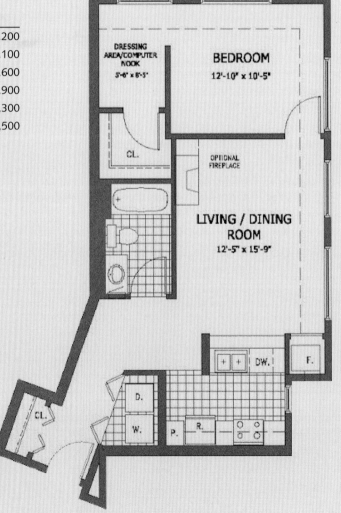

Residential Unit Information

Unit Type (Bedroom)	Number of Units	Unit Size (Square Feet)	Price Range
Studio	19	679–758	$139,200–165,200
1	34	718–837	$169,000–182,100
1 + Den	22	956–1,070	$198,100–233,600
2	15	1,191–1,482	$246,200–282,900
2 + Den	6	1,325	$272,700–287,300
2 (Townhome)	14	1,671	$303,000–329,500

Development Cost Information

Site acquisition/demolition cost	$ 6,651,500
Construction cost	19,655,800
Architectural and engineering cost	897,700
Marketing cost	2,493,600
Carrying/operating cost	1,207,400
Special consultant cost	86,900
Financing cost	538,100
Title and recording cost	178,800
Other costs	391,100
Project management fee	540,000
Total development cost	**$ 32,640,900**

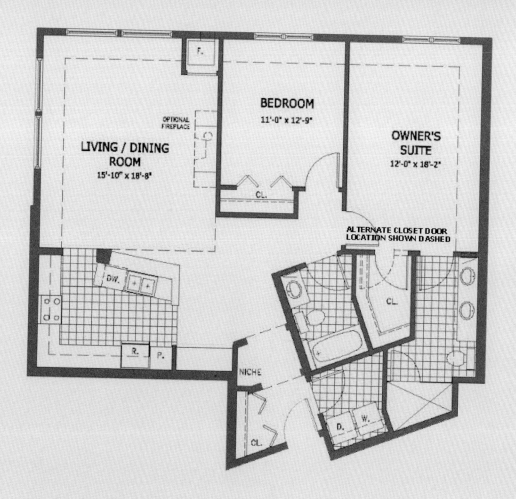

LIVING / DINING ROOM
15'-10" x 18'-8"

OPTIONAL FIREPLACE

F.

BEDROOM
11'-0" x 12'-9"

OWNER'S SUITE
12'-0" x 18'-2"

CL.

ALTERNATE CLOSET DOOR LOCATION SHOWN DASHED

CL.

DW.

R.   P.

NICHE

D. W.

CL.

Development Schedule

Market study/neighborhood process:	May 2002
Planning and zoning approval process:	November 2002
Architectural—design/development:	November 2002
Negotiate development agreement:	February 2003
Begin marketing:	April 2003
Architectural—construction drawings:	July 2003
Acquisition/relocation:	July 2003
Loan commitments:	July 2003
Bid and review process:	August 2003
Bond sale/loan closing:	September 2003
Abatement/demolition/excavation:	September 2003
Site work/utilities:	October 2003
Bond funding/construction funding:	December 2003
Construction	
Freestanding retail buildings:	October 2004
Townhomes:	November 2004
East condominium building:	January 2005
West condominium building:	February 2005
Project completed:	February 2005

Project Team

Developer
The Cornerstone Group/
  Lyndale Gateway LLC
Edina, Minnesota
thecornerstonegroup.com

Contractor
BOR-SON Construction, Inc.
Minneapolis, Minnesota
www.borson.com

Architect
Elness Swenson Graham
  Architects Inc.
Minneapolis, Minnesota
www.esgarchitects.com

Landscape Architect
Damon Farber Associates
Minneapolis, Minnesota
www.damonfarber.com

Sales
The Basil Group
Maple Grove, Minnesota
www.thebasilgroup.com

Retail Leasing and Management
Welsh Companies
Minneapolis, Minnesota
www.welshco.com

THE PALMOLIVE BUILDING

Chicago, Illinois

The 37-story art deco Palmolive Building, located at the northern end of Chicago's "Magnificent Mile" on Michigan Avenue, was originally constructed in 1929 as the headquarters of the Colgate-Palmolive Company. The first commercial skyscraper in Chicago to be built far from the Loop, the building was designed by one of Chicago's oldest and most prestigious architectural firms, Holabird & Root. The setback skyscraper was designated a Chicago landmark in 1999 and listed on the National Register of Historic Places in 2004.

The current housing boom in the Chicago area has translated to a surge in adaptive uses as developers have seized opportunities in prime locations to recycle historic office and industrial buildings into new condominiums and apartments. The conversion of the Palmolive Building to luxury condominiums follows a growth market that has been escalating since the late 1990s for high-end condominiums in downtown Chicago, with units selling from upward of $400 per square foot.

When Draper and Kramer, Incorporated (DK), a major Chicago real estate firm, acquired the Palmolive Building in 2001, the property contained two floors of vacant retail space and 35 stories of partially occupied office space. Demographic trends and market research supported an adaptive use plan to convert the historic building to 103 luxury condominiums above four floors of retail use.

The Site

Sited amid the world-class shopping at the northern end of Chicago's "Magnificent Mile," the Palmolive Building is surrounded predominantly by mixed-use, high-rise properties. Nearby uses include several thousand hotel rooms, Class A and B office space, vertical retail malls, and residential towers. Nearby landmarks include the Drake Hotel, the historic Water Tower, and the Fourth Presbyterian Church.

The upper half of the Palmolive Building offers views of Lake Michigan to the east as well as the Chicago skyline. The limestone art deco exterior contributes to an attractive residential structure. The location, architecture, and history of the building add to its market appeal.

At the time of purchase, the 30,000 square feet of retail space on the first two floors were vacant, and occupancy of the Class C office space on floors three to 37 was 70 percent, with market rent levels that had remained relatively flat for years. However, in undertaking the acquisition and development of the Palmolive Building, the developer's research indicated a strong market and significant unmet demand for luxury condominiums in downtown Chicago. An evaluation

The Palmolive Building, located
on Chicago's Magnificent Mile,
was originally completed in
1929 to house the headquarters of the Colgate-Palmolive
company. The art deco architecture includes classically
tapered limestone and brick
in the form of recessed bays,
terraced setbacks, and
decorative terra-cotta panels.
Draper and Kramer

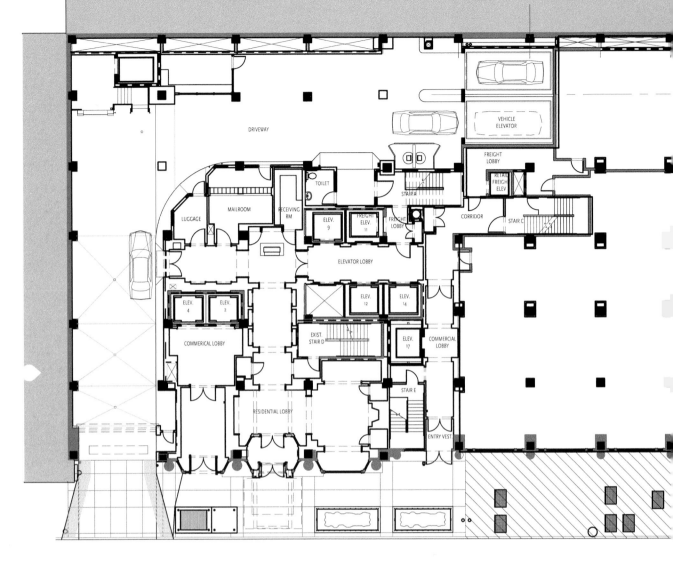

Ground-floor site plan. Booth Hansen

of the building suggested it would be a worthwhile conversion to a residential property.

Development Process

Founded in 1893, DK is a full-service real estate services firm with specialties in development, commercial mortgage, residential mortgage, asset management, pension advice, property management, brokerage, valuation, research, and insurance. Since 1950, DK has developed more than 15,000 homes and in excess of 18 million square feet of commercial space. The firm manages more than 9,000 apartments and 20,000 condominiums, mostly in the Chicago area.

Despite its long history of experience in the Chicago multifamily residential market, the renovation of the Palmolive

Building was DK's first adaptive use project. To augment its own staff in this complex redevelopment project, DK hired more than 20 independent consultants.

DK originally developed the Palmolive Building's adaptive use plan with the intention of converting only the upper portion of the building to residential use. As the development plan advanced, DK decided that only the ground floor would contain retail space, but it considered different combinations of office, hotel, and condominiums for the other 36 floors.

The timing of the property purchase—just three months before the terrorist attacks of September 11, 2001—helped sway the final decision. After 9/11, scant appetite existed for new hotel space, and the office market was soft. The final plan called for 50,000 square feet of retail and office space on

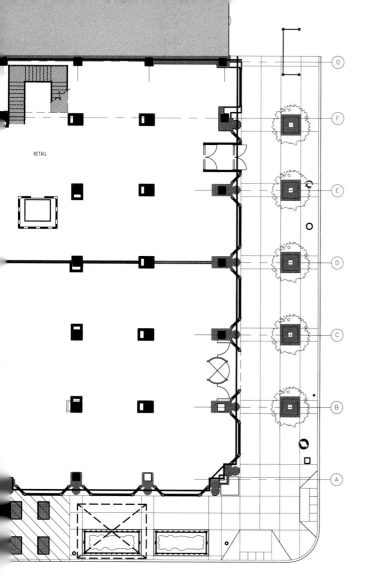

RETAIL

nate the majority of the existing leases. The purchase was financed with about 58 percent equity from DK, NEBF, and other project investors. The property was also split into two ownership entities: the retail portion, in floors one to four, and the tower portion, in floors five to 37, which also includes all common areas.

In October 2003, after reaching the lender-required 40 percent presale of condominiums, DK opened a $135 million construction loan from Corus Bank to cover 70 percent of the costs. After leasing a requisite amount of retail space, the parcel was recapitalized with an approximately 80 percent loan-to-value floating-rate debt.

Because the property was eligible for listing on the National Register of Historic Places, it also qualified for a state of Illinois real estate tax assessment freeze program available to purchasers of renovated landmark structures, subject to approval by the Illinois Historic Preservation Agency (IHPA). To receive IHPA approval of the restoration plan and the tax assessment freeze, the developers expanded the scope of the historic restoration to include two typical elevator lobbies on upper floors and the restoration of selected original interior millwork on floors 18 and 37, as well as other minor modifications to the DK plan. Participation in this program yielded a freeze on real estate taxes for condominium owners for eight years at current assessment—based on the former Class C office space with 30 percent vacancy. The property tax savings for condominium owners has been a successful marketing tool.

The project included several high-risk variables, including the adaptive use planning, construction within an existing structure, termination of existing leases, and compliance with historic reuse guidelines. The 30 percent expected rate of return, while higher than average, sought to compensate for the higher-than-average risks.

the first four floors, with 340,000 gross residential square feet (277,000 salable square feet) for the condominiums on floors five to 37. Redevelopment of the building called for completely replacing all building systems, installing loading and parking, and constructing luxury condominiums above four levels of commercial uses.

Financing

The property was offered for sale in 2000 by the lender, who had accepted a deed in lieu of foreclosure. In June 2001, DK, in partnership with its longtime pension fund partner, the National Electrical Benefit Fund (NEBF), acquired the property for $58.5 million. Acquisition financing was limited because the development plan included adaptive use and a plan to termi-

Approvals

The conversion of the property from office to residential did not pose a legal issue, since the existing zoning allowed residential use. However, the physical constraints of the existing building meant that parking could not be provided according to code. The existing lower levels presented the opportunity to add sufficient parking by using car elevators, subject to approval by the city's Planning Department. The Planning Department also approved the addition of off-street loading within the building.

Because the building is a designated Chicago landmark, the Commission on Chicago's Landmarks had to review and approve all renovation plans. Issues subject to review included modifications to the facade, roofline changes caused by mechanical modifications, the addition of French doors and railings to the terraces (designed to diminish their visual impact), the installation of planters in selected terrace locations, the replacement of existing exterior lighting, storefront renovations, and restoration of the historic interior wood carvings.

Planning, Design, and Construction

The Palmolive Building is considered an outstanding example of art deco architecture. Brick and limestone cover the classically tapered, steel-framed structure, which features recessed bays, terraced setbacks, and decorative terra-cotta panels. From 1930 to 1981, the building sported a navigational beacon, making the property a popular subject of Chicago photography.

Although the floor plates of the Palmolive Building were considered to be outdated and small for modern office usage, the many terraces, large windows, and high ceilings were found to be well suited for residential layouts. The prior office use meant the building had an ample supply of elevators, facilitating its conversion to residential use. The developer calls the concept of the renovation design "modern elegance," compatible with the historic art deco character of the building without reproducing it.

An important component of the planning process was DK's strategy for anticipating the unexpected. The firm, realizing the inevitable complications inherent in the redevelopment of an existing building, sought to allocate sufficient reserves to cover additional construction costs.

The configuration of the building and the balance between commercial and residential occupants required careful planning. An elegant residential entrance and lobby were important, while access for commercial tenants on floors two to four was also critical. First-floor tenants have street-level entries so access was not an issue for them. Although retail portions and areas reserved for residential uses, such as a private lounge and the health club, each occupied a portion of the second floor, entries to each of those areas needed to be kept separate. All elevators were replaced, the elevator lobbies were reconfigured, and a freight elevator was added off the main bank of elevators. Off-street loading and parking were required within the building but did not exist at acquisition. All of the above needed to be created while maintaining adequate fire exits.

Refurbishing storefronts to maximize the Palmolive Building's prime retail frontage on Michigan Avenue marked the project's first stage of construction. During that time, DK aggressively sought to move existing office tenants by relocating them within the building, buying out their leases, or working around them until the next phase of major construction activity. This effort strategically vacated the areas scheduled for construction while continuing to generate income from still-leasable space. The plan included the operation of temporary mechanical systems to serve tenants while replacing the old building systems.

Construction in a partly occupied structure proved complicated. The necessary demolition of the interior could not take place during the day because it would disturb ongoing tenants, while any noise from late-night demolition would be a problem for the guests of nearby hotels. Those constraints meant that interior demolition was effectively limited to late afternoon and early evening hours and progressed more slowly than anticipated.

All electrical, plumbing, and heating, ventilating, and air conditioning (HVAC) systems required replacement because the original 1929 building systems were still in place and functionally obsolete. In an effort to avoid an overhead HVAC distribution system that would likely encumber the interiors with soffits to disguise ceiling-mounted ductwork or create clumsy, two-foot-deep window sills to hide appliances, the developer spent almost two years testing and developing an under-floor system that houses ductwork below living space. New fire systems were installed, including the addition of sprinklers throughout the building.

DK sought to maximize the building's existing assets while integrating new, top-of-the-line improvements in the renovation. The developer chose to market the units with luxury-level standard finish packages, rather than charging buyers more for upgrades. Buyers may also choose to purchase the units unfinished—a trendy option at some very high-end properties that allows property owners to create a custom interior in decorator-ready raw space.

Allowing for substantial customization of the units as part of the conversion of the building included designing the MEP (mechanical/electrical/plumbing) system with sufficient latitude to permit flexibility in each unit's layout. As a result, many buyers have made substantial alterations to their condominium's floor plans. DK has provided architectural services to assist with those modifications.

DK hired Booth Hansen Associates as the project architect, a well-regarded firm with significant experience in creating luxury homes as well as in situating new design inside historic buildings. Booth Hansen led the complex, multiyear endeavor to produce the custom design and detailing that accompanied the complete renovation of the building, particularly for the

The 37-story skyscraper towers above the Drake Hotel, offering bird's-eye views of Lake Michigan, Lake Shore Drive, and Michigan Avenue.

Draper and Kramer

new condominiums. Advisory consultants commented on and helped refine the plans.

The renovation plan for contributing historic features included significant repairs to and careful cleaning of the landmarked limestone facade and decorative terra-cotta spandrel panels. Although no additions or modifications were permitted to the facade, the residential entry doors and vestibule are newly designed with a nickel canopy that is reminiscent of the building's original storefronts. DK also decided to repair the historic beacon mast and revive the former beacon with the installation of a World War II–era model.

Condominium unit sizes range from 1,146-square-foot one-bedroom units to 13 full-floor, 5,400-square-foot units, as well as a 7,880-square-foot duplex penthouse occupying the top two floors. Unit prices start at $450,000, and the penthouse, at $10.7 million, qualifies as the city's most-expensive condominium listing ever. The upper-level luxury units, at an average price of more than $4 million, have the best and most-expansive views and include generous terraces of up to 2,300 square feet.

Standard finishes include walnut double entry doors, four-inch-wide white oak flooring, stone and marble fireplaces, gourmet kitchens, floor-to-ceiling slab limestone in master baths and powder rooms, extensive millwork, and custom details in the 9^1/$_2$-foot ceilings. Kitchens are equipped with Wolf, Sub-Zero, and Miele appliances.

The new building systems include some of the most advanced residential technology available, including a touch-screen system for residents to call for their cars from the garage, to receive notification of deliveries, and to provide easy communication with the building's services and staff, which include a 24-hour concierge and doorman. Other amenities include common areas consistent with luxury condominiums, such as a private lounge and health club, and a valet garage offering a weekly car wash.

The three basement levels contain 150 private valet parking spaces and an interior loading area. Ten spaces are reserved for the retail tenants and 140 spaces are set aside for condominium owners. The condominium parking factor of 1.4 spaces per unit, while lower than optimal, is considered adequate.

The building's Michigan Avenue frontage is consistent with Chicago's landscape ordinance, which requires trees along the public right-of-way. The project team selected the Princeton Sentry gingko for the street trees, for both its hardiness to withstand Chicago's snowy winters and the delicate canopy that does not impose on the retail facades. The landscaping

The lobby of the Palmolive Building was restored to evoke the original 1929 design with walnut paneling, nickel metalwork, and stone floors.
Draper and Kramer

on the building's Walton Street side includes in-ground side-walk planting beds with custom-painted steel rails and black granite borders, designed to reflect the historic and deluxe character of the neighborhood. In addition, seasonal plantings diversify the landscaping throughout the year.

Marketing and Management

The developer was compelled to respond to the unstable real estate market conditions that emerged immediately following September 11, 2001, which markedly slowed high-rise residential sales in many major American cities, including Chicago. In light of those changes in the marketplace, DK found it necessary to postpone its development plan for the Palmolive Building by more than a year and wait for consumer confidence to return and restore the market for luxury tower condominiums.

With a property located in a district with one of the highest median incomes in the Midwest, DK launched a condominium marketing campaign to sell an ultraluxury development to wealthy buyers. This strategy included providing a unique product maximizing the landmark property's desirable location and spectacular views, enhancing its architectural appeal, and designing a high-quality amenity package that would meet the expectations of the target market. Providing luxury finishes as standard has also proven very successful for marketing the Palmolive, because it fulfills the expectations and preferences of high-end buyers. Other premium features included the views on the upper floors and the overall quality of the redevelopment. The result was price points near the top of the market, ranging from just under $400 per square foot for a smaller unit on the lower floors to more than $1,300 per square foot for a terrace home with spectacular city views.

Standard luxury finishes in the condominiums include stone and marble fireplaces, extensive millwork, and other custom details. Draper and Kramer

The developer focused marketing efforts on direct marketing and cooperating brokers, augmented by a dedicated Web site and print advertising in high-quality publications, such as *Chicago* magazine, *Chicago Social, North Shore Magazine,* and *Architectural Digest.* Signage was also placed at the site, although city code limited its size and placement.

In addition to the in-house production of promotional materials, an advertising firm assisted with the development of print advertising and high-quality brochures with artistic renderings of key areas. Direct mail invited prospective buyers to open-house cocktail parties in the model residence. DK also prioritized Realtor relations, hiring two of the most experienced upper-end real estate brokers in the city to work exclusively for the development and offering Realtors attractive cooperating commissions and payment terms.

The marketing strategy especially sought to demonstrate to prospective buyers that Class C office property could be transformed into luxury residential property. The developer launched residential sales at the Palmolive Building in November 2002 with the construction of a temporary model lobby entrance, and a 5,400-square-foot full-floor model residence and an on-site sales office to highlight the finishes and architectural design. Later, two more fully furnished models and a model interior hallway were added.

The first sales of the 103 condominium units closed in fall 2005, and DK expected all units to be sold out by fall 2006. Brokers secure 70 percent of buyers. Most of the buyers are professional couples, many of whom are empty nesters. A majority, 75 percent, are Chicago residents; in fact, many already lived within a close radius of the Palmolive Building. Other purchasers are from the suburbs or out of town.

DK, as the largest condominium property management company in the city, will continue in that role after all of the residential units have been sold. Extensive easements and rights of access describe the rights of both the condominium owners and the retail parcel owners, allocating responsibilities and shared costs between them.

The retail space with frontage on Michigan Avenue is now successfully leased to two new upscale flagship anchors. In February 2003, Louis Vuitton opened a 7,400-square-foot storefront. In June 2003, St. John Knits opened a 9,500-square-foot two-story store. The Elizabeth Arden Red Door Salon & Day Spa, a preconversion retail tenant that continued to operate through the construction phase, remains on the fourth floor. The Private Bank has opened its Gold Coast branch on the second floor. One remaining previous office tenant, a dentist, is also part of the retail/office portion of the property, having relocated to the third floor. The retail rents compare favorably to other Michigan Avenue retail spaces, after adjustment for location, size, and other factors. In August 2005, the California-based Michigan Avenue Retail LLC, owned by Ross Hilton Kemper, acquired 50,000 square feet of the Palmolive Building's retail space for $54 million, or approximately $1,100 per square foot.

Experience Gained

DK carefully tracked and responded to the slowing market following 9/11 and the later demand boom, successfully converting the Palmolive Building into luxury condominiums.

» Have a vision. Renovating one of Chicago's most recognizable and architecturally distinguished buildings to its former eminence and reinventing it as a residential tower required long-term vision from the developer—especially in light of the complications from September 11, 2001. In particular, 9/11 was a deciding factor in the choice of predominantly residential as the conversion use. Other possible uses that were originally considered, such as hotel space, were less marketable right after 9/11.

» In adaptive use, plan for the unexpected. Recognizing that rehabilitation is often more difficult than new construction and anticipating the complexities related to working within an existing structure, DK set aside substantial reserves during the planning stages. In doing so, the developer sought to provide adequate reserves to fund unknown future costs. Nonetheless, necessary but unforeseeable facade repairs still exceeded expectations, and certain structural conditions that were not apparent on the original plans or were not revealed during the initial investigations also contributed to a shortfall in the budgeted reserves.

» Strong relationships are important. The developer's long-standing and trusted relationships with its primary investor and the lender helped the firm ride out the ups and downs of the project, particularly the rocky market conditions immediately following 9/11. After September 11, 2001, sales of high-rise condominiums in Chicago slowed dramatically. The development plan was delayed by more than a year as DK reacted to the changes in the marketplace and waited for investor confidence to return.

Two-bedroom residence.

Booth Hansen

» Capitalize on a property's inherent advantages. Despite the challenges presented to the market and economic environment after 9/11, the property's highly desirable location and unique historic architecture still offered a solid foundation for the success of the development.

» Vacate existing tenants before beginning construction. Not all the existing office tenants in the Palmolive Building were willing to move, so DK devised a strategy to work around them. However, this approach slowed down demolition considerably, because the issue of noise disturbing current tenants sharply curtailed daytime demolition activity.

» A high-quality finish package can be a good marketing tool for a high-end luxury residential product. Rather than offer standard midlevel finishes and compel buyers to pay more for upgrades, the developer and architect assembled a high level of standard finishes to meet the target market preferences. As a result, purchasers receive a good value because of the developer's bulk purchase of these luxury materials.

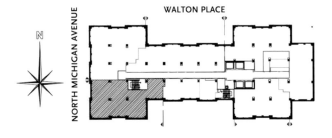

Project Data: Palmolive Building

www.palmolivebuilding.com

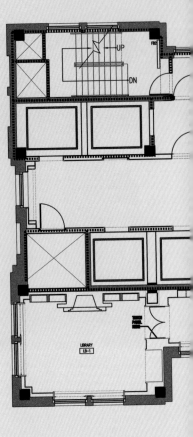

Land Use Information

Site area: 28,000 square feet

Total dwelling units planned: 101

Total dwelling units completed: 55

Land Use Plan

High-rise condominiums

Development Cost

	Retail	Condominium
Building acquisition	$ 19,500,000	$ 39,900,000
Construction costs	11,800,000	107,500,000
Soft costs	1,600,000	10,400,000
Operating costs	4,800,000	28,800,000
Financial costs	4,500,000	8,300,000
Total development cost	**$ 42,200,000**	**$ 194,900,000**

Residential Unit Information

Unit Type (Bedroom/ Bath)	Number of Units	Unit Size (Square Feet)	Price Range
1/1	15	1,146–1,278	$453,375–798,000
2/2.5	50	1,529–2,832	$674,000–2,010,000
3/3.5	22	2,912–4,732	$1,569,000–6,100,000
Full floor (3–4/3.5–4.5)	13	4,292–5,400	$4,320,000–6,200,000
Penthouse (3/5.5)	1	7,880	$10,624,000
Total	**101 (planned)**		

Development Schedule

Site purchased:	May 2001
Planning started:	June 2001
Construction started:	October 2003
Sales started:	November 2002
First closing:	November 2005
Project completed:	December 2006 (projected)

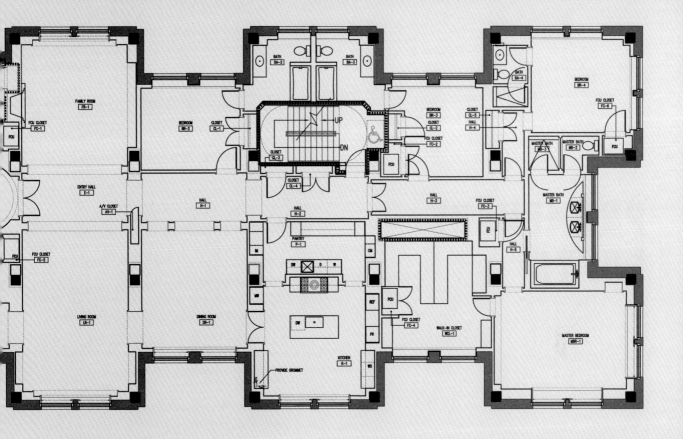

Project Team

Developer
Draper and Kramer,
    Incorporated
Chicago, Illinois
www.draperandkramer.com

Architect
Booth Hansen Associates
Chicago, Illinois
www.boothhansen.com

Structural Engineer
Thornton & Tomassetti
Chicago, Illinois
www.ttengineers.com

Exterior Facade Contractor
Berglund Construction
Chicago, Illinois
www.berglundco.com

**General Contractor
(Interior Finishes)**
Pepper Construction
Chicago, Illinois
www.pepperconstruction.com

**General Contractor
(Base Building)**
Walsh Construction
Chicago, Illinois
www.walshgroup.com

Landmarks Consultant
Baldwin Historic Properties
Chicago, Illinois

Exterior Facade Engineer
Horvath Reich CDC, Inc.
Chicago, Illinois

Construction Consulting
The RISE Group, LLC
Chicago, Illinois

Full-floor residence.
Booth Hansen

PROMENADE LOFTS

Denver, Colorado

When the Promenade Lofts was completed in 2002, the project marked a milestone for the city of Denver as well as the developer, East West Partners. The 66-unit condominium building and two adjacent buildings were the first residential development in a long-abandoned rail yard next to the South Platte River.

East West Partners acquired 23 acres along the river in 1999. At the time, many people viewed the property as a wasteland and could not imagine why anyone would want to live there.

For years, Denver struggled to redevelop the area, known as the Central Platte Valley. The land is within walking distance of the city's financial district, and civic leaders wanted development that would make a dramatic statement about the city and help revive downtown.

To change the character of the area, the city of Denver tore down several dilapidated buildings along the South Platte and built 25-acre Commons Park, directly across the street from Promenade Lofts. Plans were also made to extend the city's 16th Street pedestrian mall to the river, with a dramatic 28-foot suspension bridge carrying foot traffic over the remaining rail line and into a public square that would become a focal point for the new development.

Promenade Lofts was an immediate success. East West Partners was soon breaking local records for sales prices, and the firm began making plans for hundreds of additional units of townhomes, condominiums, and apartments. Today the firm is building a 23-story condominium tower just down the street from the Promenade Lofts.

The area, now known as Riverfront Park, has become a popular place to live. A bike path along the river links residents to Coors Field and Denver's other sports stadiums, as well as the Denver Performing Arts Complex and the popular Lower Downtown historic district, often referred to as LoDo.

An area once regarded as an eyesore on the edge of downtown is now one of the city's most prestigious addresses. At buildout, East West Partners expects Riverfront Park to have 2,000 to 3,000 units with a value of over $1 billion.

The Site

Over a 30-year period, dozens of proposals were floated for the land that became Riverfront Park, including turning all of it into a public park, building a new convention center there, and creating a suburban-style office park.

Denver was hit hard by a regional recession in the late 1980s, and a glut of office space downtown brought a halt to most development schemes. To try to revive downtown's

Promenade Lofts, a seven-story condominium and retail tower, set and maintained local pricing records even in the post-9/11 recession. Julie Hutchinson/Thin Air Studio

Easy access to Denver's Lower Downtown was a key selling point for Promenade Lofts buyers. Julie Hutchinson/ Thin Air Studio

fortunes, the city created the Lower Downtown historic district in the old warehouse area next to Union Station, the city's historic rail terminus. The district quickly became a hit with the public, and many of the large commercial warehouses were renovated into residential lofts.

The success of Lower Downtown made clear that a market existed for urban-style living in Denver, a city that had seen most development go to the suburbs in the decades following World War II. The empty land along the South Platte River was immediately north of Union Station and just a few blocks from Lower Downtown.

However, several obstacles impeded development of the property. For years it had been thought of as a no-man's land, and several run-down storage buildings blocked access to the river from downtown. The still heavily used rail tracks behind Union Station also acted as a barrier to the property.

Development Process

The ownership of the land had changed hands several times before finally being consolidated by Trillium Corporation in the early 1990s. Trillium began working with the Denver city government on a zoning plan for the area, with the goal of creating an urban village that would include hundreds of new residential units, as well as retail and office buildings. The city acquired the land along the river for Commons Park and also began work on extending the city's 16th Street pedestrian mall into the area, eventually building a dramatic pedestrian bridge over the railroad tracks that linked the property to the rest of downtown. Known as the Millennium Bridge in honor of the new century, the bridge features a large mast that is illuminated at night and has become a new downtown landmark.

Most of the difficult work in rezoning the property and planning for utilities, roads, and other amenities was already done when East West Partners bought the land from Trillium. Trillium never saw itself as a developer, but rather it always planned to sell the land to an entity with real experience building communities. By assembling all the property and getting it zoned, Trillium made the property far more valuable. "The city of Denver and Trillium had already gone through the zoning process," said Chris Frampton, director of sales and marketing for East West Partners. "What we bought already had a PUD [planned unit development]. In essence, we bought a master plan."

Creating Riverfront Park marked a dramatic departure for East West Partners. The firm had made a name for itself building high-end condominium projects at Colorado ski resorts, including Vail and Beaver Creek. East West Partners built the Hyatt Regency hotel in Beaver Creek and worked on dozens of other projects in mountain communities.

Harry Frampton, the managing partner of East West Partners, heard former Denver mayor Wellington Webb speak about the potential of the Central Platte Valley at an Urban Land Institute conference in 1998. That sparked the firm's interest in doing a project in one of the most urban sites in Colorado.

Financing

Total costs for the Promenade Lofts were nearly $29 million. Construction cost $21.6 million, while soft costs—including architectural fees, legal expenses, marketing, and other services—added another $6.1 million. The land acquisition for the site cost $586,500. Site improvement costs were $519,000. The cost per unit of land acquisition for 66 units was $8,886.

Because of East West Partners' solid record of success in the mountains, the firm was able to tap into an already established network of investors. Its financial partner is Crescent Real Estate Equities, a real estate investment trust based in Fort Worth, Texas.

"At the time of that project, equity requirements were 25 percent, and the lion's share of equity was provided by Crescent," said Amy Fuller, chief financial officer for East West Partners–Denver. Fuller said the remaining equity was provided by the partners within East West Partners.

Construction financing was provided by Bank of America and was guaranteed by Crescent. The loan agreement required that 50 percent of the units be presold before construction.

Fuller said that East West Partners typically aims for a 15 to 20 percent return on investment in its projects.

The costs of building the Millennium Bridge over the rail tracks, as well as the roads, sidewalks, and other amenities, were handled by the city of Denver through the creation of a metropolitan district. The bonds the district issued to fund those costs will be paid back through property taxes collected from the new development. By using this method, known as tax increment financing, Denver was able to fund the infrastructure without asking taxpayers for support.

Planning and Design

The design of the Promenade Lofts was crucial to the success of the overall development because the building and its two sister loft projects would be the first built in Riverfront Park. Additionally, the buildings would surround a public plaza at the base of the Millennium Bridge, marking the end of the 16th Street Mall and providing a gateway to Commons Park. The buildings were guaranteed a highly visible place in the civic landscape, with hundreds of people walking by on their way to and from downtown.

East West Partners wanted an architectural style that would link Riverfront Park to the much-loved red-brick warehouses of Lower Downtown while also giving the area its own identity. "The design goal was to have something that reflected the character of LoDo but has its own character," said Chris Frampton. "One of the things we realized is that Riverfront Park has a unique position and is contiguous to the city."

Architect Randy Johnson of Denver's 42/40 Architects chose a design palette that included an earthy red brick that calls to mind the century-old buildings in LoDo. He also added horizontal detailing by recessing some of the bricks, as well as using other colors in brick and stone to make the facade compelling. "Masonry was a big deal," said Frampton. "That mixed brick gives a depth to it and makes it visually interesting." Nevertheless, the building is unambiguously contemporary, with floor-to-ceiling windows in many units and a distinctive sandstone-faced, round, two-story structure that provides residents with direct access to the Millennium Bridge.

The Promenade has 49 one-bedroom units, ranging from 880 to 1,568 square feet, 12 two-bedroom units from 1,440 to 1,934 square feet, four three-bedroom units ranging from 2,457 to 3,276 square feet, and one enormous four-bedroom penthouse that sprawls over 4,149 square feet. All of the units have generous balconies, and many have sweeping views of downtown or the mountains. In deference to the popularity of the nearby lofts in LoDo, East West Partners chose to give its units a classic, loftlike feel, with exposed concrete columns and ducts and glass tile in the bathrooms.

The building is next to a busy freight line that often hosts long coal trains passing through Denver. Frampton said care was taken to buffer residents from the inevitable noise. "The railroad tracks were a concern at first," he said. "We did a lot of construction stuff to mitigate that." Glazing was added that would block noise and an acoustical barrier was built into the brick fence that lines the tracks. The garage in the building includes a concrete wall filled with rubber to buffer the noise from the tracks.

Nevertheless, East West Partners eventually came to accept the railroad as part of the urban landscape. Frampton says some potential buyers were turned off by the rumble from the rail yard, but others thought it was part of the fun of living downtown.

"I think people recognize trains are part of an urban neighborhood," he said. "There's a romance to it. People understand that's part of the Denver experience."

An eclectic mix of materials energizes the building's exterior and helps integrate the structure into the diverse mix of commercial and residential buildings nearby. Julie Hutchinson/ Thin Air Studio

To give Riverfront Park a unique ambience, East West Partners sought out local retailers rather than national chains. Julie Hutchinson/Thin Air Studio

Expanses of glass provide sweeping views of the South Platte River and downtown Denver. Julie Hutchinson/Thin Air Studio

DEVELOPING CONDOMINIUMS

Marketing and Buyers

Because the Promenade marked the debut of a whole new district of downtown Denver, East West Partners knew that the marketing would set the tone for the public's overall perception of Riverfront Park.

The easy access to downtown was a key selling point, but the company also pitched Riverfront Park as a distinct area with access to nature, unusual in an urban setting. "The message was 'This is Denver's Central Park neighborhood,'" said Frampton. "It's contiguous to downtown but not in it."

The company also worked to remind potential buyers of the many new attractions added to downtown Denver in recent years, including several new sports stadiums, an expanded performing arts center, and dozens of new restaurants and nightclubs in Lower Downtown. "We wanted people to understand how great downtown was," said Frampton. "We wanted to say, 'Look at all the stuff going on. It's fun.'"

The company targeted two kinds of buyers: single people who worked downtown and people who lived in the mountains but came to Denver frequently on business. "We had a lot of people in the mountains who knew East West Partners and came to Denver a lot," said Frampton. "They needed a single bedroom and a good kitchen. They wanted a cozy, comfortable living space and maybe a second room that could be a bedroom or an office."

From the moment marketing began, sales were brisk. "That building did really well," said Frampton. "It sold incredibly quickly." East West Partners sold 80 percent of the units very quickly, then September 11, 2001, and the recession hit. The final 20 percent took longer to sell. Downtown Denver was booming in those years, and many projects sold quickly, but Riverfront Park was seen as more desirable than other locations.

Although sales dropped during the recession that began in 2001, East West Partners was still able to set local records in pricing. While units in Lower Downtown at the time were selling for $250 per square foot, units at the Promenade were going for $330 a square foot.

Frampton says the company realized a real demand existed for downtown living in Denver. Although Denver's downtown has always been a major office center, until recently little housing has been available in the city center.

"There's a great statistic that Denver has 140,000 people who work downtown and only 8,000 people who live here," said Frampton. "We felt like there was pent-up demand, but you can't find it overnight."

Management

East West Partners has kept ownership of the first floor of the Promenade and the two adjacent buildings, which are devoted to retail. A coffee shop, a wine store, two restaurants, a bank, a pet shop, and other retailers occupy that space. A nonprofit art gallery brings in temporary exhibitions. The company has intentionally sought out local retailers rather than national chains, trying to give the area a special ambience.

The Promenade has a homeowners association (HOA) that owns and maintains the common areas in the building. Riverfront Park has a master association that cleans and maintains community areas, including many of the streets and public plazas. Each building's HOA makes a contribution to the master association, which is run by the developer.

Experience Gained

Even though Promenade Lofts was an unqualified success, Frampton says East West Partners would do a few things differently.

» The target market was slightly different than originally projected. Initially, the company designed the building as a timeshare, thinking a large demand for small units would come from people who spent a couple of weeks a year in Denver. The company soon discovered that most of its buyers intended to live in the building, and 80 percent of the residents now live there full time. "It was started with the idea it would be timeshares, but the end result didn't reflect that," said Frampton. The developer built more one-bedroom units than it might otherwise have done (49 of 66 units).

» For many buyers there can never be too many windows. "We built too long and narrow, a classic developer mistake," said Frampton. "We found people like more windows. People wanted more natural light." That is not likely to be problem with the firm's latest project at Riverfront Park. Now under construction, that 23-story condominium tower will be almost entirely faced with glass and is known as the Glass House.

Project Data: Promenade Lofts

www.promenadelofts.com

Land Use Information

Site area: 22,522 square feet

Total dwelling units: 66

Total parking spaces: 272

    Retail 190

    Sold with units 72

    Commercial 10

Gross density: 127.65 units per acre

Average net density: 127.65 units per acre

Land Use Plan

	Square feet	Percentage of Site
Mixed-use*	22,522	100

*Residential, retail, parking: First floor is retail, floors 2 to 7 are residential, parking is underground and on level 1.

Residential Unit Information

Unit Type (Bedroom/ Bath)	Number of Units Built	Unit Size (Square Feet)	Range of Final Sales Prices
1/1.5	49	880–1,568	$274,900–699,000
2/2 or 3	12	1,440–1,934	$436,900–849,900
3/2 or 3	4	2,457–3,276	$899,000–1,499,000
4/3.5	1	4,149	$1,650,000

Development Cost Information

Land acquisition cost	$ 586,500
Site improvement cost	519,000
Construction cost	21,612,000
Soft costs	6,124,800
Total development cost	**$ 28,842,300**

Development Schedule

Site purchased:	1999
Planning started:	1999
Construction started:	June 2000
Sales started:	April 2000
First closing:	January 2002
Phase 1 completed:	January 2002
Project completed:	January 2002

Project Team

Developer

East West Partners–
    Denver, Inc. (dba Park Plaza
    at Riverfront Park LLC)
Denver, Colorado
www.ewpartners.com

Site Planner

AJ Zabbia
68 West Engineering, Inc.
Denver, Colorado
www.68west.com

Architect

Randy Johnson
42|40 Architects
Denver, Colorado
www.4240arch.com

General Contractor

MA Mortenson
Denver, Colorado
www.mortenson.com

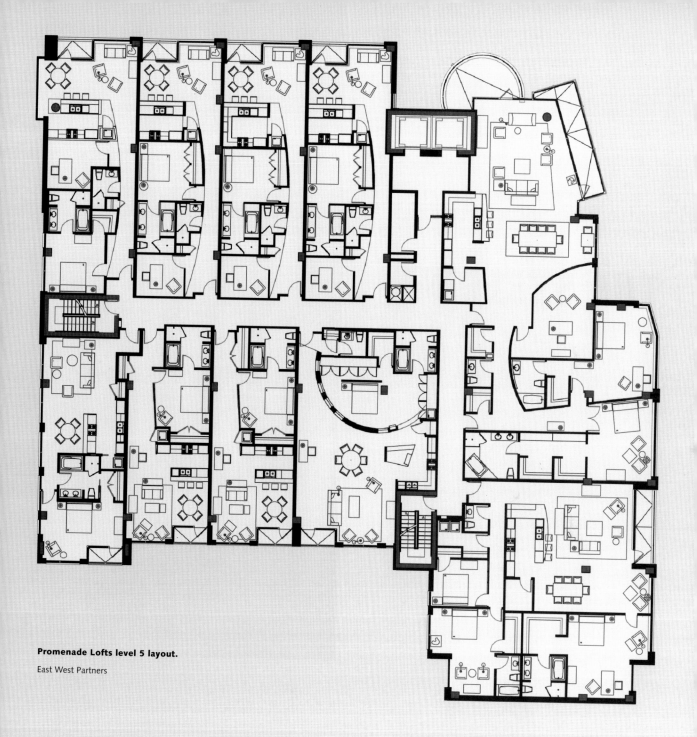

Promenade Lofts level 5 layout.

East West Partners

THE STELLINA

Seattle, Washington

The Stellina added 34 affordable one- and two- bedroom condominium units to Seattle's hot housing market while, at the same time, healing a neighborhood that had served as a staging ground for highway construction for more than three decades. Inspired by a group of community activists, non-profit developer HomeSight partnered with the city of Seattle to offer new housing choices for blue-collar and service workers who would not otherwise be able to purchase homes in the area.

The intensely sloping site challenged the construction and design teams, but it affords excellent views of the Olympic

Mountains and Mount Rainier, Beacon Hill, and downtown Seattle. The new condominiums, priced at appraised market rates, were made available to qualified first-time buyers through a purchase assistance package including deferred payments, amortized low-interest loans, and property tax savings passed through to buyers. This package made the Stellina affordable to workers and families with incomes as low as 36 percent of the area's median income and to people who could not previously afford to buy a home in Seattle's Central Area.

HomeSight, a nonprofit developer, partnered with a group of community activists and the city of Seattle to create a new housing opportunity for blue-collar and service workers who would not otherwise be able to purchase homes in the area.

Clair Enlow

The Site

The Jackson Place community lies southeast of downtown Seattle and just north of a new Interstate 90 interchange. Thirty years of planned and actual highway construction, beginning in the 1960s, turned the neighborhood into a giant staging ground for heavy construction. By the 1990s, a small but effective core of activists emerged. Angered by the resulting disruption, doubt, and depopulation, the group was determined to knit the fabric of the neighborhood back together. As a nonprofit developer, HomeSight has partnered with those citizens and with the city of Seattle since 1990 to replace lost housing and revitalize Jackson Place.

Meanwhile, in the late 1980s, the combination of a hot housing market and the proximity to downtown Seattle threatened Jackson Place with gentrification and loss of ethnic and economic diversity. To protect the community, the city purchased land declared surplus from the state and county in order to pursue its affordable housing agenda. The site, later to be the

Below: Although the intense slope of the Stellina site challenged the construction and design teams, it affords excellent views of the Olympic Mountains and Mount Rainier, Beacon Hill, and downtown Seattle. Clair Enlow

The Stellina was a pilot project for Washington state's "Affordable by Design" program. Dedicated to encouraging lower-priced and attractive high-density residential projects in urban growth areas, the designation carries a grant of $175,000 to help with project financing. HomeSight (facing page)

Stellina's home, was assembled by the city from a combination of the newly purchased land and privately held property.

The triangular, 40,698-square-foot lot occupies approximately half of a block just to the north of Interstate 90 and near the intersection of two major arterials, Jackson Street and Rainier Avenue. It slopes steeply down toward the commercial and light industrial Rainier corridor, which runs south from Seattle's International District all the way to the southern city limit.

In addition to two neighborhood streets at the perimeter of the block, the lot is bounded by city right-of-way over the 68-year-old Cedar River water main, a five-foot-diameter pipe running diagonally under the middle of the block. The slope had become a de facto dumping ground for waste and debris during highway construction, and it was littered with large and small pieces of concrete among brush and scattered trees.

Occupying the northwest, downhill side of the block, on the other side of the water main, is a multistory co-housing community. The community was built around a garden court in the late 1990s on surplus land also sold by the city. Across the street along the uphill side of the block is a poorly renovated, four-story apartment building that dates from 1919. Blocks on the uphill side are occupied primarily by single-family houses.

The site is well located for residents who do not have a car. It is near the International District within a few blocks of downtown Seattle's free-ride zone for Metro buses. The I-90 bike path and Judkins and Pratt parks are nearby.

Development Process

HomeSight is a nonprofit community development corporation dedicated to the production of for-sale housing that is affordable to first-time buyers who would otherwise be priced out of the housing market. Founded in 1990, HomeSight began by building freestanding single-family homes on scattered sites. The organization moved on to a full-scale development of more than 30 houses on underused land in Seattle's Central Area, with concurrent construction of streets, utilities, sidewalks, gutters, and curbs. At the time the Stellina was completed, in 2004, HomeSight had developed and sold more than 300 new units; in 2006, it had more than 100 units under construction.

As a developer, HomeSight places a priority on using locally owned building subcontractors and has developed a reputation for excellent construction quality and energy efficiency along with affordability. In keeping with its mission of providing homeownership opportunities for city dwellers with low-to-moderate income, HomeSight offers financial assessment and education as well as down payment assistance and low-interest loans for prospective buyers. The nonprofit developer and its missions are supported through public and private foundation grants, program-related investments, and fee-for-service charges.

The Stellina is the first condominium for HomeSight's development team, led by Nora Liu and Uche Okezie. Each of HomeSight's projects is influenced by community input. Earlier projects reflect the desires of low- and moderate-income

A purchase assistance package, including deferred payments, amortized low-interest loans, and property tax savings passed through to buyers, made the Stellina affordable to workers and families with incomes as low as 36 percent of the area's median income. Clair Enlow

families to own a single-family home, while the Stellina reflects the community's desire, especially among those members without children, for smaller condominium units.

The group acquired the site when the city of Seattle issued a request for proposals (RFP) for housing on the site in 1999. The RFP stipulated that at least 50 percent of the units produced would be affordable and that the design would be consistent with neighborhood goals and responsive to concerns in the neighborhood. With its record of delivering nearby housing according to those criteria, HomeSight was selected as the purchaser and developer of the land.

Subsequently, the Stellina was selected during the planning stages as a demonstration project for the Washington State Department of Community, Trade, and Economic Development's "Affordable by Design" housing pilot program, which is dedicated to encouraging affordable and attractive high-density residential projects in urban growth areas. In addition to prestige, the designation carries a grant of $175,000 to help with financing the project.

The P-Patch Program of the Department of Neighborhoods, in conjunction with the not-for-profit P-Patch Trust, provided community garden space for residents at the Stellina. Supporting a strong environmental ethic, the P-Patch Program allows only organic gardening. P-Patch gardeners show their concern for the value of fresh organic vegetables by supplying seven to ten tons of produce to Seattle food banks each year. Because of high demand, only one plot per household is available.

Financing

The $6.1 million construction cost of the Stellina was financed with a $3.6 million loan from Homestreet Bank at 0.25 percent above the prime lending rate. The Local Initiative Support Corporation (LISC), a national nonprofit community development financing corporation, provided a subordinated loan of $950,000. The rest of the package included a $175,000 demonstration project grant from the state and a $150,000 grant from NeighborWorks America (a congressionally chartered redevelopment network). HomeSight was able to provide the equity for the remaining $1.2 million.

HomeSight helped in seeking conventional loans for buyers. City of Seattle restrictions on sale of the land required that at least six units be sold to households with incomes equal to or less than 80 percent of area median, which is now set at $40,600 per year for a one-person household in the Seattle metropolitan area. Over half of the buyers at the Stellina were qualified by household size. Those buyers were able to borrow up to $70,000 each from a city of Seattle loan pool of $954,000 that had been designated for HomeSight to use within the city of Seattle. According to the terms of those loans, repayment of principal and interest (at 3 percent) is deferred for eight years, with interest payments starting in year nine and principal payments starting in year 30. In addition to a loan from city funds, those buyers were able to borrow up to $70,000 each in funds from HomeSight's Puget Sound Revolving Loan Fund at below-market interest, for a total low-interest loan package of up to $140,000. The city of Seattle has also granted a ten-year property tax exemption on improvements, an exemption passed on to buyers.

Approvals

Land for the Stellina was purchased from the city of Seattle in accordance with an ordinance promoting housing ownership choices for low-to-moderate-income people and encouraging compatible infill development in areas affected by highway construction. As buyer and developer, HomeSight was able to leverage its position and reputation for successful redevelopment projects during the approval process, assembling a team of city staff people from the Seattle Department of Planning and Development, the Seattle Department of Transportation, Seattle Public Utilities, and the Seattle Office of Housing. These staff members were able to work with HomeSight to expedite the permit application from the preapplication phase through approval.

In the process of partnering with the city, the Stellina became a testing ground for several regulatory changes, including a pilot height variance. Previous regulations tied maximum building heights to irregularities and depressions in the existing, partially excavated grade. Taken to the logical extreme, very irregular ground could produce a highly irregular roof slope. HomeSight requested and tested a more practical application of height limitation, based on the naturally curving grade that extends to and includes the curvature of perimeter streets.

Another variance provided a model for minimizing the scope of work for sidewalks, curbs, and gutters and for creating better conditions for the involvement of private contractors in those projects. For example, it allows the use of private surveyors in right-of-way work and the designation of a single point of contact to ensure consistency from design through construction oversight by the city's department of transportation.

Partnership with a team of city staff people expedited problem solving on the complex site. Instead of seeking approval for a complicated easement on its property alongside the water main, HomeSight simply deeded the entire 14-foot-wide strip of land alongside the water main (nearly 5,000 square feet) to the city.

Design

To use the difficult site to its full potential and deliver the maximum number of condominium units practical, HomeSight turned to architect Ronald Vigil of R.G. Vigil Architects. Vigil responded to the 40 percent slope and spectacular views of Mount Rainier, downtown Seattle, the Rainier Valley, and surrounding hills by setting three two-story condominium structures, each containing eight units, atop a long, contiguous parking garage cut into the hillside. A separate building on the lower, tapering end of the site contains another ten units.

Washington state law mandates 5 percent of the units in a multifamily structure without elevators be accessible for the handicapped. Therefore, two of the Stellina's ten units in the lower structure are "Type A," or fully wheelchair accessible.

In addition, the ground-floor units in one building along the street on the uphill side of the lot are "Type B" accessible, meaning that the entrance, corridor, and doorways are adapted to wheelchair use.

Units are "efficient" in size. One-bedroom condominiums are 600 square feet and two-bedroom units are 760 square feet, with the two Type A accessible units somewhat larger. They are arranged in sets of eight, in symmetrical floor plates with four units on each floor. Each four-unit floor plate includes two two-bedroom units that wrap around two one-bedroom units, with living/dining rooms oriented toward views. The same total floor area occupied by each set of eight units is divided into just two accessible units in the lower level of the ten-unit building.

The three upper structures are on top of, but back from the edge of, the concrete parking structure on the view side to accommodate individual decks, which are divided from each other with trellis structures. Upper-level units open out to the view with balconies off the living rooms. Except in the top-floor units, which have cathedral ceilings in the living/dining rooms and eight-foot-high ceilings in the remaining areas, the remaining units have nine-foot-high ceilings throughout.

The structure of the Stellina is standard wood frame, slab on grade for the lower building and wood frame over concrete parking structure in the larger, three-section upper building. Preengineered materials helped keep construction costs down. Setting unusually tight standards for moisture content in lumber (3 percent) minimized shrinkage in structural members and cracking in drywall.

While the common, mirror-image unit plans and repetitive floor plates lend important economies to the design and construction, all those features also work to break down the bulk and perceived scale of the Stellina. Exterior elevations gain more dimension with window bays on the front, back, and sides. Finally, the fiber cement board siding takes three traditional forms—board and batten, lap siding, and shingles—that are arranged on exterior walls to further articulate facades. A repeating four-color paint palette distinguishes the siding textures.

Marketing and Management

Because of historically low prices and lingering depression of land values following highway construction in the neighborhood, market-rate prices for the condominium units were low by Seattle standards, ranging from $152,000 to $220,000.

Marketing and sales of the units were handled by a local real estate agent who has consistently worked with HomeSight projects and clearly understands the developer's agenda of reaching out to local, low-to-moderate-income buyers. The agent, Jada Pettigrew, developed special expertise in locating, prequalifying, and supporting moderate-income buyers in working with previous HomeSight projects. She also mailed postcards, held open houses, and placed sandwich boards on the curb.

Neighborhood involvement in project planning paid off for HomeSight. Awareness and community ownership led to a high proportion of buyers with family ties in the diverse communities of the surrounding blocks.

Sales at the Stellina began in fall 2004, and the last unit sold about one year later. The typical buyer at the Stellina is a single woman in her 20s or 30s, but men and retirees, as well as one family of four, have also purchased units. Occupations include teachers, flight attendants, social service employees, housekeepers, and restaurant workers. Some income-qualified buyers hold more than one job.

HomeSight's condominium declaration includes covenants, conditions, restrictions, and reservations typical for market-rate condominium sales. In accordance with the declaration, owners have formed a condominium association to cover costs and manage maintenance of the gardens, courtyards, garage, and building shell. All units are individually metered for water and electricity.

Seattle's P-Patch Program provided community garden space for residents at the Stellina. P-Patch gardeners supply seven to ten tons of organic produce to Seattle food banks each year.

Clair Enlow

Experience Gained

Departing from its focus on single-family home development was a positive learning experience for HomeSight.

» Condominiums are attractive to a broad market. Condominium ownership, which has been increasingly associated with affluent young professionals and retirees living in downtown Seattle, is also attractive to those with limited incomes. In fact, condominium living is a very desirable option for many first-time buyers with moderate incomes.

» Developer choices can influence buyer financing. Some first-time buyers find that their chosen lenders require the development to meet the comprehensive underwriting standards of the Federal Housing Administration (FHA). HomeSight did not seek FHA approval, thinking that Federal National Mortgage Association approval would be sufficient for mortgages. FHA underwriting standards are more inclusive.

» Favorable relationships must be maintained with city staff members. Working with city agencies and utility companies is essential in managing costs, especially on environmentally sensitive sites and those requiring improvements to streets, side-walks, and utility connections. The HomeSight team met with a designated set of city staff members to agree on goals and solutions for the project, assign task lists, and coordinate schedules. However, the development team did not engage the electrical utility until the optimal time had passed, and as a result, delays were caused by awkwardness in sizing and placing a transformer vault as well as associated poles and lines.

» The cost of insuring a condominium development is escalating. The Stellina is sided with fiber cement board, a durable, long-lasting material increasingly used instead of exterior insulated fastening systems (EIFS) (manufactured stucco siding). Even though the project did not use EIFS, HomeSight paid a total of $350,000 in condominium liability insurance (over $10,000 per unit) for the Stellina. This cost resulted from steep rises in the cost of insuring condominiums, which correlate with court cases involving water damage and the failure of EIFS. HomeSight believes that in order to encourage construction of condominiums as an affordable housing alternative, nonprofit and for-profit developers should lobby for reform in this area and consider creating a pool of insurers.

Project Data: The Stellina

Land Use Information

Site area: 40,698 square feet

Total dwelling units: 34

Land Use Plan

	Square feet	Percentage of Site
Attached residential	20,416	50.1
Common open space	17,125	42.1
Small parking lot and sidewalks	3,157	7.8
Total	**40,698**	**100.0**

Residential Unit Information

Unit Type (Bedroom/ Bath)	Number of Units Built	Unit Size (Square Feet)	Range of Sales Prices
1/1	16	555	$159,000–173,950
2/1	16	755	$181,500–215,000
1/1 ADA	1	975	$177,000
2/1 ADA	1	1,101	$195,000

Development Cost Information

Site acquisition cost	$ 123,500
Site improvement cost	416,600
Construction cost	2,388,100
Soft cost	2,687,500
Total development cost	**$5,615,700**

Development Schedule

Site purchased:	June 2003
Construction started:	August 2003
Sales started:	June 2004
First closing:	October 2004
Phase 1 completed:	October 2004
Project completed:	November 2004

Project Team

Developer
HomeSight
Seattle, Washington

Site Planner and Architect
Ron Vigil
Seattle, Washington

General Contractor
Buchanan General Contracting
Bellevue, Washington
www.buchanangc.com

Civil Engineer
Del Erickson
Bellevue, Washington

Geotechnical Engineer
Geotech Consultants
Bellevue, Washington

Real Estate Agent
VelDyke Realty, Inc.
Seattle, Washington
www.veldykerealty.com

The Stellina's view of Seattle's nighttime skyline (facing page). HomeSight

One- and two-bedroom floor plans. HomeSight

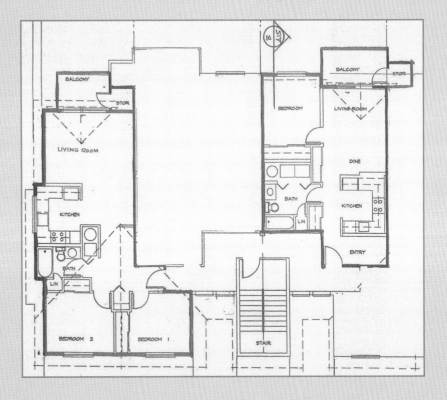

THE TERRACES AT EMERYSTATION

Emeryville, California

For most of the 20th century, the city of Emeryville, in Alameda County, California, hosted primarily industrial uses—paint manufacturers, warehouses, rail lines, and steel mills. Industry began declining in the 1970s, prompting the city to spearhead environmental cleanup and concentrate on attracting computer and biotechnology corporations as well as shopping centers and housing. Completed in 2003, the 150,000-square-foot Terraces at EmeryStation is a key part of the city's renaissance, part of a larger mixed-use village surrounding an active intermodal transit station.

The Terraces includes 101 traditional and loft condominium units in five stories above a four-floor (700-car) above-ground parking structure. Located on a brownfield site adjacent to the Emeryville Amtrak Capitol Corridor Station, the building is the third phase of the master-planned Emery-

Built on a brownfield site, the Terraces is located next door to the Emeryville Amtrak station, the first new train station built in California in more than 60 years, providing a much-needed rail facility linking San Francisco with Sacramento and points beyond. Heller Manus Architects

Station, following on the heels of two mixed-use office buildings. The developer's goal was to create an attractive design that would reflect the city's industrial roots while providing an inviting place to live.

The Site and History

Emeryville is located at the foot of the San Francisco Bay Bridge, between Berkeley and Oakland, less than ten miles from downtown San Francisco. Now primarily known as a center for software and biotechnology corporations, the city has seen demand for housing increase as its economic strength has improved. Incorporated in 1896, the city for most of the 20th century was an industrial and manufacturing center for the Bay Area. In the last two decades, with the demise of those sectors, artists began moving into the spacious loft-type spaces, which

were, for a time, affordable. Emeryville's redevelopment agency has encouraged new uses, and within the last few years an array of housing types, office buildings, a regional mall, a big-box mall, and an IKEA have been developed.

As a transit-oriented development, the Terraces offers excellent connections to a variety of transportation options. The access ramp to Interstate 80 is less than a mile to the west, providing easy access to the Bay Bridge and San Francisco. In addition, the multinodal Amtrak station is a transit hub and provides connections to numerous Alameda Contra Costa Transit bus lines as well as the free Emery Go Round shuttle bus connecting to BART. A pedestrian bridge crosses over the railroad tracks to connect the residences to EmeryBay, a major mixed-use development that includes retail, offices, apartments, and the restaurants of the EmeryBay Public Market.

The 150,000-square-foot Terraces at EmeryStation is a key part of a larger mixed-use village surrounding a San Francisco Bay–area transit hub. Five stories of traditional and loft condominium units sit above a four-floor parking podium to limit noise from the railroad line and an adjacent thoroughfare. Heller Manus Architects

The Amtrak train station opened in 1993 as the western terminus of the California Zephyr from Chicago. It has since become the eighth-busiest Amtrak station in the country. The EmeryStation master plan created a mixed-use development with two office buildings: EmeryStation One, completed in 1999, is a five-story, 384,000-square-foot office building; EmeryStation North, completed in 2001, is a six-story, 200,000-square-foot office building; both have retail and parking on the ground floor. The Terraces at EmeryStation is bounded by EmeryStation One across Horton Street to the east, the Amtrak station to the north, the Union Pacific railroad tracks to the west, and the overpass for Powell Street—a major boulevard—to the south.

The site is flat, with no existing vegetation prior to the development. Like most areas of Emeryville, this site had housed industrial uses, most recently a Chevron tank site and a Westinghouse Corporation transformer factory, both abandoned for well over a decade. As a result, the site required extensive environmental remediation. The site's previous owner, Viacom (Westinghouse's successor), removed a portion of the soils contaminated with PCBs as well as underground tanks. The development team for the Terraces then constructed an asphalt cap over the remaining PCB-contaminated soil, building the parking podium for the Terraces on top of that.

Development and Financing

San Rafael–based Wareham Development has been involved in real estate development and property management in the Bay Area since 1977. It has been actively involved in Emeryville's postindustrial transformation. Two of the firm's earliest projects were completed in Emeryville in 1980: Hollis Street Center, the first industrial building in the Bay Area to be legally converted to artists' lofts and studio residences, and Heritage Square, which houses offices and laboratories. The company's commercial developments include life-sciences, high-technology, industrial, and retail tenants, and residential properties. Wareham Development retains ownership of the majority of its projects.

When Amtrak sought to establish a train station in Emeryville, Wareham built the station on land leased from the city and master planned the EmeryStation development around it. For the Terraces, Wareham entered into a joint venture with Thompson Dorfman, a Sausalito-based real estate development and investment firm founded in 1999 that offered expertise in multifamily housing, particularly in the areas of product, programming, and sales strategy implementation. Wareham and Thompson Dorfman Partners, LLC, created a single-asset entity for this project. The challenges of working with a contaminated site were outweighed by the site's desirable proximity to a major intermodal transportation

The residential floors are configured in a U shape, creating a central, landscaped courtyard. On the east side of the building, the condominium units step back, creating the terraces that give the building its name.

Heller Manus Architects

119

Perched atop the parking structures, condominium units
provide excellent views: on the
eastern edge of the building,
units look to the Berkeley Hills
and the University of California
at Berkeley, while on the
western edge, units face San
Francisco Bay. Heller Manus
Architects

hub in Emeryville's most active business, entertainment, and retail area.

The joint venture of Wareham and Thompson Dorfman owns 50 percent of the Terraces (with 40 percent belonging to Wareham, 10 percent belonging to Thompson Dorfman) while Prudential owns the other half. Prudential provided a guarantee for the construction loan from Guaranty Federal Reserve Bank, providing 100 percent financing. Wareham owns the parking structure over which the residential units were built and contributed as its equity the air rights above the parking. The city had already approved the parking structure and granted Wareham the right to build 101 units. In addition, Wareham signed a guarantee to take responsibility for any shortfalls during construction that exceeded construction financing. Thompson Dorfman did not make a financial contribution.

Legal Issues

The state of California requires that local governments incorporate "fair share" housing production goals into their general plans, to ensure that each region as a whole creates sufficient affordable housing to meet its needs and that each city has a role in providing affordable housing. The Association of Bay Area Governments establishes those requirements for Bay Area cities. To meet Emeryville's regional fair-share housing goals, as established in its Affordable Housing Ordinance, 20 percent of the units were sold at below-market rates to low-income homebuyers. Some below-market-rate homebuyers received financial assistance from the local government in addition to low-interest mortgages. The below-market-rate units are under a deed restriction, so those homebuyers receive a limited annual appreciation based on the consumer price index when they sell their units. All units, both market rate and below market rate, are finished in the same way.

The developers worked with both the Emeryville planning commission and the city council during the approvals process. The dialogue with the city influenced the amount of terracing and the form of the building. The terracing reduces the apparent bulk of the building, creates outdoor spaces for the residents, and gives the building a more interesting and distinctive profile. It also responds to the terraced design of the other buildings at EmeryStation. Wareham did not require any unusual approvals; however, the standard process lasted longer than is typical while Wareham watched the housing and office markets to see whether offices might be a better use for the Terraces site. During that time, construction on the parking garage portion of the project was begun.

Planning and Design

Heller Manus Architects of San Francisco designed the building's shell, and MVE & Partners of Irvine, California, designed the interiors. Heller Manus Architects had already designed the Amtrak station, EmeryStation One, and EmeryStation North. The brick facade of the parking structure complements the brick of the two office buildings, recalling the look of 19th-century train stations.

Because of the proximity of the railroad line and the Powell Street overpass, any housing placed at grade would suffer from noise and unappealing views. At the same time, the two office buildings of EmeryStation required extensive parking. The solution was to create a four-story podium for parking, raising the residential units above the busy thoroughfare and railroad line. In order to provide parking for the office uses immediately, the parking structure was finished before construction of the residential portion began. As a result, the architects had to design the parking structure to support the residential component before the residences had received final approval and their final form had been determined.

To respond to the streetscape, the parking structure is clad in brick along its lower levels on the north and east sides, facing the rest of EmeryStation, to relate to the brick facades and detailing of the complex's other structures. The sides facing the Powell Street overpass and the railroad tracks, which have little public visibility, are clad in concrete. On all four sides, the building's upper levels have concrete and stucco facades.

Above the parking podium, the building takes the shape of a U, creating a landscaped courtyard. On the east side of the building, the two levels above parking and the three top levels step back, creating the terraces that give the building its name. The courtyard includes palm trees and a water feature, serving as an oasis in the high-density urban setting. All of the buildings at EmeryStation have a significant amount of green space, and the Terraces benefits from views down to the landscaped courtyard across the street at EmeryStation One. Because of the placement on top of the four-story parking structure, units have excellent views—on the eastern edge of the building, units look to the Berkeley Hills and the University of California at Berkeley; on the western edge, units face the bay, the Bay Bridge, and Mount Tamalpais across the bay in Marin.

Residents enter the Terraces from the main entrance on Horton Street. An elevator leads to the parking levels and the courtyard on the parking structure's roof. Occupants then walk across the courtyard to reach the residential lobby, where another set of elevators provides access to the units above. Amenities include a fitness center, saunas, locker rooms, a conference room and business center, a private movie theater, a parking garage, private landscaped terraces off the lobby entrance, and a resident clubhouse available for functions. The Terraces has two layers of security: security guards monitor both the parking garage at street level and the residential lobby on the fourth floor.

Units consist of a mix of studios, one- and two-bedroom flats, one- and two-bedroom lofts, and one-bedroom penthouses. Based on 11-foot floor plates (22-foot floor plates in the lofts), the units range in size from 587 square feet to 1,823 square feet. To maximize natural light and views, large floor-to-ceiling storefront-type windows allow light to penetrate even into units that are located deep within the building. Many of the units have balconies, which along with high ceilings and contemporary open floor plans contribute to the building's spacious feeling. Operable windows provide natural ventilation. Gourmet kitchens feature granite countertops, stainless steel appliances, and gas ranges. The industrial loft design encouraged a number of residents to have their own custom design work performed on their units.

The building's concrete structure consists of round columns fashioned from Sonotube, cylindrical forms made from many layers of high-quality fiber, spirally wound and laminated with a special adhesive. Exposed, unfinished concrete columns and square caps complement the industrial style of the surrounding area. The massing of the parking structure serves as an effective vibration damper when trains pass by. Double-pane windows and thick insulation also protect the units from noise.

Originally the project was designed for fewer units, but subsequent redesigns increased the unit count by reconfiguring the interiors, making the units smaller and reducing the variety of units to simplify construction.

The first two levels of parking are assigned to EmeryStation One and Two across the street. Wareham leases parking on the third and fourth levels to owners of the condominiums. Developing subterranean parking for the EmeryStation One and Two office buildings would have been prohibitively expensive because of the adjacent San Francisco Bay and the high water table. Congregating the parking for the office and residential uses in one above-ground structure was financially viable and gave the residential units views of the hills to the east and the water to the west.

Marketing and Sales

In 1999, the for-sale market was not as strong as the rental market. However, the development team decided that the project should be designed to function as either a rental community or a for-sale condominium community. This approach gave the owners flexibility to respond to changing conditions in the housing markets over the course of the design, entitlement, and construction phases. The program reflected the similarity between target residential markets for both luxury rental and for-sale properties.

As it turned out, six months before construction was complete, the condominium market was much stronger than it had been, and interest rates seemed likely to remain low. Therefore, the owners decided to sell the units as condominiums. During construction, the owners began the process of registering the units as condominiums with the city and the California Department of Real Estate. Although the plans and infrastructure were not altered, the finish options were upgraded, including the fixtures and tile in the bathrooms, the granite countertops, and wood cabinets in the kitchen. In addition, soundproofing in the units was improved. The Terraces was completed in 2003 and sold out completely at prices 10 percent higher than projected. The average sales price per unit for the market-rate housing was $430,400. Average sales price per square foot was $375. Wareham used standard signage and newspaper advertisements to market and sell the units. Other media were not necessary because sales proceeded faster than expected, the project selling out in less than one year.

Part of the reason for the project's success is that approximately one-quarter of the units were designed as lofts, a highly popular option in Emeryville, which is known for its many industrial buildings that have been converted into artists' lofts and live/work studios.

Buyers have chiefly consisted of young professional singles and couples, and homeowners who have recently retired or who are preparing for retirement.

Experience Gained

Creativity and flexibility helped the developers turn minor roadblocks into inventive opportunities during development of the Terraces.

» Do not foreclose future opportunities. The Terraces illustrates the value of designing multifamily housing to be flexible enough to serve as either apartments or condominiums. Depending on the strength of the rental market compared to the for-sale market during construction, the units can be finished appropriately to meet the needs of the market.

» Flexibility does not need to increase cost. The dual approach does not have to add significantly to construction costs. Upgrading the finishes to the level appropriate for condo-

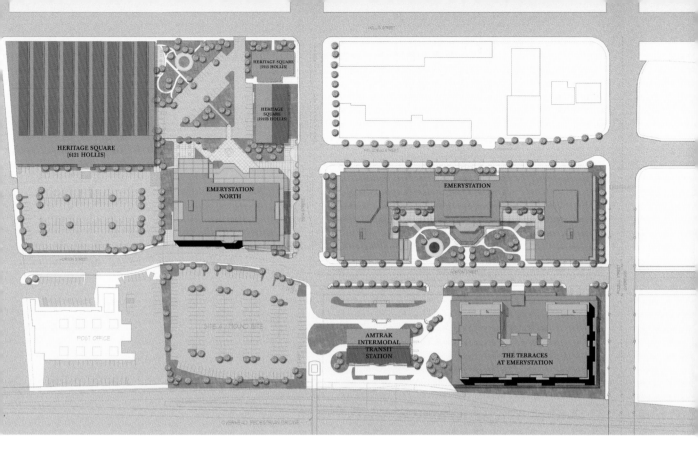

miniums did add some expense. However, many finishes are typically left to the homebuyers in condominium sales anyway: in this case, buyers could choose to upgrade flooring and lighting if they wanted. The only other significant additional expense was that of mapping the property to prepare it for condominiums, a process that would have likely been performed even if the units were sold as rentals, allowing for the possibility of future conversions to condominiums.

» A tight infill site can provide an opportunity to be creative. Creating a combined parking structure to serve both the office buildings and the condominiums was an excellent way to make use of limited space on the site, the high water table, and the remediated land; to raise the residences above the noise of the train tracks and busy overpass; and to take advantage of views. This approach could prove useful in similar urban neighborhoods where space is constrained and traffic or train noise is an issue. Building the parking structure first enabled the offices to start using the parking as soon as possible, before the residential portion was completed.

EmeryStation (above) and master plan (top). Heller Manus Architects

Project Data: The Terraces at EmeryStation

Land Use Information

Site area: 1.0 acres

Total dwelling units: 101

Total parking spaces: 700

   Office 599

   Residential 101

Land Use Plan

Use	Acres
Buildings and parking	1.0

Residential Unit Information

Unit Type (Bedroom/ Bath)	Number of Units	Unit Size (Square Feet)	Range of Sales Prices
Studio	4	587–611	below market rate
1-bedroom flat (junior)	8	633	below market rate
1-bedroom flat	8	749	$295,000–345,000
1-bedroom penthouse	4	823	$335,000–375,000
1-bedroom flat + den	23	861–1,001	$295,000–395,000
1-bedroom loft	8	1,068	$355,000–406,000
Studio loft	4	1,277	$398,540–415,000
2-bedroom flat	26	1,080–1,226	$261,950–473,000
2-bedroom loft	16	1,512–1,823	$500,000–610,000
Total	**101**		

Sales Prices

Average sales price/unit (market rate): $430,400

Average sales price per square foot (market rate): $375

Homeowners association dues per month: $419

Development Cost

Land and fees	$ 1,000,000
Hard cost	20,000,000
Soft cost	7,500,000
Sales and marketing	2,000,000
Financing cost	1,500,000
Total cost	**$ 32,000,000**

Development Schedule

Construction started:	Spring 2001
Sales started:	Summer 2003
First closing:	Winter 2003
Project completed:	Spring 2004

Project Team

Developer

Wareham Development

San Rafael, California

www.warehamdevelopment.com

Joint Venture Developer

Thompson Dorfman Residential
   Partners, LLC

Sausalito, California

www.thompsondorfman.com

Architect (Shell and Core)

Heller-Manus Architects

San Francisco, California

www.hellermanus.com

Architect (Interiors)

MVE & Partners

Irvine, California

www.mve-architects.com

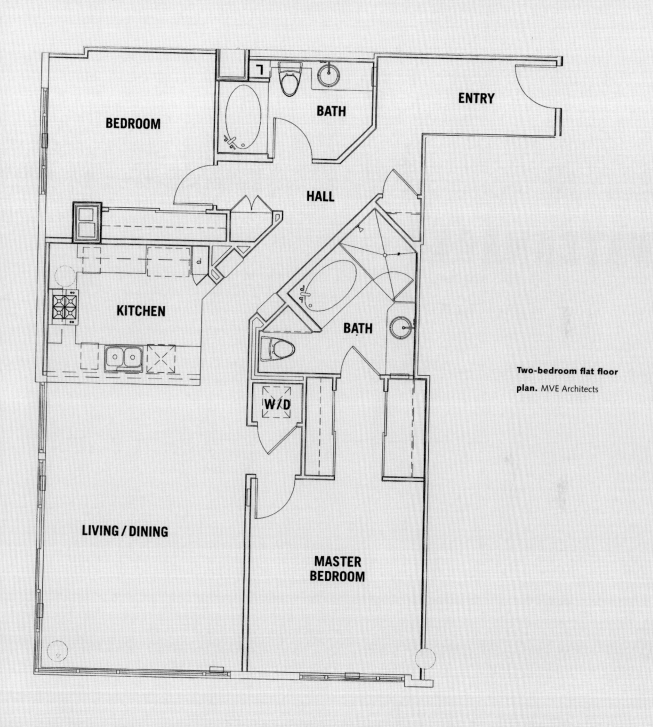

BEDROOM

BATH

ENTRY

HALL

KITCHEN

BATH

Two-bedroom flat floor plan. MVE Architects

W/D

LIVING / DINING

MASTER BEDROOM

WATERMARKE

Irvine, California

Built on the fringe of a mixed-use metropolis and permanently protected open space by the Sares·Regis Group (SRG), the Watermarke community was originally intended as rental units but was later switched to condominiums. The 535-unit luxury multifamily community was designed to surpass all comparable projects in the city of Irvine, California, at a time when the region was dominated by one sizable development company exercising a massive budget. The northern European architecture set the community apart from the Mediterranean style that prevailed throughout Irvine and adjacent Newport Beach. A single building design (four stories of residential units on grade, connected at each level to a multistory on-grade parking structure that is hidden by the condominium buildings) is copied on the property, creating two nearly identical sets of structures and common areas.

Watermarke was mapped as a condominium development at the time of its original entitlement. The project consists of two nearly identical condominium buildings and a centralized clubhouse. Condominium buildings are referred to as Building A, which includes 256 units, and Building B, which includes 279 units. Each building was divided into 12 individual sales phases. Phases 1 through 6 were designated in Building B and phases 7 through 12 were designated in Building A. Building A was built first and was originally operated as rental condominiums. Midway through construction, the market was demanding for-sale product, which encouraged SRG to sell the units as condominium homes. This change allowed SRG to create a new partner, Watermarke LLC, to buy Watermarke from the partnership that originally owned the project and start selling the unoccupied units as condominiums. The project was extraordinarily successful, selling out in 12 months.

The Site

Irvine is located in southern California, immediately adjacent to Newport Beach and about an hour south of Los Angeles. With a population of 170,567 and a median income of $72,057, Irvine is one of California's most affluent cities. *Money* magazine repeatedly rates Irvine among the top ten places to live, and the city has topped the FBI's list of the safest cities in America with populations over 100,000. In addition, Irvine is considered the fifth-best city for women, according to the *Ladies' Home Journal*.

Opportunities for recreation and entertainment abound in the area surrounding Watermarke. More than 500 restaurants, 100 movie screens, nine golf courses, six resort hotels, five live-performance theaters, and 14,000 acres of public parkland are located within a six-mile radius of the property. Immediate

Watermarke, a 535-unit luxury condominium community in Irvine, California, blends vacation-style living with urban convenience and permanently protected natural areas. Responding to Orange County's booming condominium market, developer Sares·Regis Group made a midconstruction switch from rental to for-sale product.

Sares·Regis Group

access to Interstate 405, Orange County's principal north-south freeway, puts downtown Los Angeles as few as 50 minutes away. Amtrak service is available from the nearby Irvine train station, with links to coastal California cities. California Routes 55 and 73 (Toll Road) provide additional connections within ten minutes of the site, and California Route 1, known as Pacific Coast Highway, runs along the coastline ten minutes from the property.

The enormous business and industrial centers at Irvine Business Complex, Irvine Spectrum Center, and South Coast Metro are minutes away. The county's legal and governmen-

tal center at Santa Ana is 15 minutes away, and the University of California at Irvine (UCI) campus is one mile from the site, providing abundant educational, research, and employment opportunities.

Noting the valuable location, SRG acquired the land for $36 million in 2001. Watermarke sits one block from the city limits of Newport Beach, at the intersection of Campus Drive and Carlson Avenue in Irvine, just southeast of Jamboree Road and Campus Drive. Primary access to the ten-acre Watermarke site is by a pedestrian-friendly, brick-paved and tree-lined entry drive off Carlson Avenue, one block east of Jamboree Road.

The project's signature entry avenue, named Watermarke Place, establishes the community's presence and creates a sense of arrival. The site is bordered to the north and east by a condominium project being developed by Opus West. Watermarke balances its urban convenience with the rare opportunity for outdoor recreation and scenic vistas. Southeast of the site is the San Joaquin Freshwater Preserve, which is maintained by the Irvine Ranch Water District, and the UCI arboretum borders the southwest edge. The 568-unit Toscana Apartments, an upscale community built in 1989, wraps the eastern edge.

Development Process

During the 1960s and 1970s the site and adjacent area were home to a Beckman Instruments industrial plant that produced eye surgery equipment. The plant shut down in the late 1970s and Prudential Financial, Inc., bought the entire area. In the 1980s, the Mola development company purchased the vacant site, promising a mixed-use development dominated by new office construction. That development never occurred because of the decline in demand for office space in the late 1980s and early 1990s as well as legal disputes regarding the remediation of the toxicity Beckman's plant left behind. Mola later sold the land back to Prudential, which held on to it for several years before selling it in parcels during the early 2000s.

SRG is a real estate firm focused exclusively on the western United States. Since 1975, SRG has acquired, developed, leased, and managed an assortment of real estate, including multifamily, office, warehouse, research and development, and retail. The firm currently operates more than $1.5 billion in real estate assets, specializing in multifamily residential investment, industrial investment, development, and management.

SRG bought two tracts of land from Prudential in December 2000—one for multifamily residential development and the second for an office development. The firm later decided to sell the second site because of a lack of demand for office space in the Irvine area.

At the time the Watermarke site was purchased, Mediterranean-style apartments dominated the area's residential development. To stand out in the sea of pastel stucco and tile roofs, SRG became aggressively creative. The firm chose innovative features, such as on-grade wrap-style parking—where the residential buildings completely surround and are connected to the parking garage on every level—highly detailed floor plans, and an assortment of vacation-style amenities to establish the project's competitive edge.

SRG originally targeted the high-end rental market at Watermarke; however, a market study encouraged SRG to sell the units as condominium homes. The switch was not a condominium conversion because SRG maps and entitles all of its multifamily residential projects as condominiums at the beginning of the development process. The company adopted this policy in order to maximize long-term flexibility and to create greater value in its products. Since Watermarke was originally designed as a high-end, luxury apartment community, it required few stylistic updates to be suitable for condominium sales.

The delayed decision to sell Watermarke as condominiums did create an overlap between renters and buyers. Renters began moving into Watermarke's Building A (256 units) in October 2003 and were notified of SRG's intention to sell their units as condominiums in September 2004. Tenants were given the option to buy their units, with various tenant and as-is discounts, or to vacate at the end of their lease. This process was facilitated by a series of legal notices and a clause in each rental agreement stating that Watermarke was owned as a condominium community and could be sold as individual condominiums at any time.

Design

Gated for limited access, yet connected to the amenities that surround it, Watermarke creates an urban oasis for its residents. The modern European architecture, characterized by rounded arches, slender columns, iron-railed balconies, large wall areas filled with windows of varying sizes, syncopated roof peaks, and courtyards with lush gardens and fountains, stands out among scores of Mediterranean-style apartment communities throughout Irvine and adjacent Newport Beach. A single building design (four stories of residential units on grade connect at every level to multistory on-grade parking structures) is mirrored on the property, creating two identical sets of structures and common areas. The buildings are served by elevators, and all units are accessible by handicapped people. Most units' assigned parking space(s) are located on the same level as the unit. Rooftop recreation sundecks are set upon one of the two multilevel parking structures.

The buildings are designed to take maximum advantage of the natural views that adjoin the site on two sides. The residences ribbon around open-ended courtyards, creating eight separate outdoor environments that break up the units and provide 60 percent of condominium owners with views of the natural areas. Maximizing the number of units with views maximized the sales revenue.

A central entrance avenue, an administrative and recreation building, and a pool area separate the two residential structures. Rhythmically spaced architectural elements and

Watermarke's resort-style design is anchored by a central spine featuring an 8,000-square-foot clubhouse (above), a junior Olympic-sized pool, a spa (staffed with an aesthetician and a masseuse), and a fitness center. Sares·Regis Group

The modern European architecture is characterized by rounded arches, slender columns, iron-railed balconies, windows of various sizes, syncopated roof peaks, and courtyards with lush gardens and fountains.

Alexa Bach

two-story townhomes create an attention-grabbing facade, eliminating repetitive rows of identical windows. Select units have oversized windows, French doors, and Juliet balconies. Single-level homes with a variety of one-, two-, and three-bedroom layouts occur on all levels throughout the community, as do the townhomes. The main entry drive into Watermarke emulates an upscale, urban streetscape. Two-level townhomes adjoin a tree-lined avenue, each with its own half-flight front stoop, encouraging pedestrian activity. The avenue ends at a cul-de-sac directly in front of the 8,000-square-foot clubhouse. Beyond the clubhouse, a junior Olympic-sized pool, spa, and deck provide a focal point for the property. The main pool is offset by two smaller satellite pools with fountains imported from England. SRG chose an interior designer with extensive experience in hospitality projects to provide residents with the vacation lifestyle at home. As a result, Watermarke's common areas resemble those of a five-star hotel.

The recreation and fitness facilities are located at the far end of the pool, creating the ambience of a deluxe resort. A spa, staffed with an aesthetician and masseuse, is located within the fitness facility. The poolside cabanas can be reserved for relaxation or for an outdoor massage. On-site concierge service is available daily to provide assistance to residents with transportation, housekeeping, pet care, party planning, event ticketing, and other business and leisure needs. The Watermarke concierge also coordinates its well-attended social events, including cooking and yoga classes, wine tastings, and luaus.

Consistent with the uptown lifestyle, Watermarke's floor plans are named for landmark residential venues in America's capital of sophistication, New York City—including Fifth Avenue, Dorchester, Gramercy Park, Astor Court, and Embassy Row. The diverse selection of nine floor plans met the needs of the broad target market. Entry-level one-bedroom units, dual master two-bedroom units, spacious townhomes, and dramatically designed three-bedroom corner units are some of the floor plan highlights. Interior design and artwork reflect a classic Park Avenue lifestyle.

Standard interior appointments and finishes include hardwood-style laminate flooring, upgraded carpet, gas fireplaces, nine-foot ceilings, oversized windows, exterior doors, and built-in office alcoves and media/art niches. Buyers were able to customize their homes by purchasing an assortment of upgrades for kitchen appliances, countertops, and bathroom fixtures, such as separate tub and shower stalls and double sinks. Residents further personalized their space with design elements, including glass-block wall accents, ceiling fans, mantels, and oversized walk-in closets.

Because Watermarke was originally designed as a high-end luxury apartment community, it already included many of the design features usually added for a condominium conversion. Such details included basic granite countertops (owners could upgrade to different colors and styles of granite), crown molding, large and multifaceted floor plans, and washers and dryers. In addition, the units rented as apartments in Building A (phases 7 through 12) were only ten months old at the time of transition, so the floors, cabinets, and appliances were practically brand new. A few common-area amenities were updated, including an extensive corridor-improvement program that enhanced paint, concrete, entry lighting, and finish carpentry work at each unit's entry door, along with stucco detailing and installation of new chandeliers at the stairwell lobbies. The elevator lobbies in the parking garage were upgraded prior to condominium sales. Additionally, at the request of a buyer, two apartments were combined into a single condominium home. A one-bedroom, one-bathroom with den unit was joined with a three-bedroom, two-bathroom unit to create a 2,280-square-foot condominium suite.

Construction

SRG's construction team dealt with the poor, silty, clay soils and the high water table natural to the area but did not run into any problems with either. Facilitating fire department access in and around the tight site was more troublesome. In order to accomplish this, the team decided to construct concrete tunnels on the ground floors of the buildings. The tunnels enable firefighters to enter the parking garages without worrying that a burning building could fall on them in the process. The tunnels also blend with the project's architecture.

The city of Irvine required a landscaped wall on the southern corner of the property. Meeting this requirement was difficult because of the grade of the land, but the construction team created a mechanically stabilized wall using a geogrid system to reinforce the earth. The project was required to provide certain amenities to satisfy the city's park ordinance (and avoid a city of Irvine park fee). The tight site did not provide enough space for all of the amenities to exist on the same grade; therefore, a double-deck sports facility was created. The very expensive, but very popular, structure includes a ground-level basketball court with a tennis court on top. The court has been so popular that people have been known to travel up to 40 miles just to play there, and Watermarke's security guard has had to shoo away members of the public, trespassing and climbing over the gates to use the courts. The two-level sports facility is shared with Toscana, the mid-rise apartment community bordering the northeast edge of Watermarke. Equity Residential's position as an investor in Watermarke and owner of Toscana alleviated any

SRG created a double-deck sports facility to provide all the amenities required by the city of Irvine. The expensive but popular structure includes a tennis court over a ground-level basketball court. Alexa Bach

potential red tape during design and construction of the shared facilities.

The on-grade wrap-style parking was challenging but successful. To make the parking garages invisible from outside the community and to provide unit-level access to all homeowners, the construction team tied the wood-framed buildings to the concrete parking structures at every story.

Financing

Total costs for developing Watermarke were $153.1 million. Development of the apartment community cost $116.2 million, and the condominium transformation added an additional $36.9 million (including the cost of condominium transformation and the price for completing Building B). SRG originally acquired the site for $34.6 million and spent $10.7 million on

The southern edge of Watermarke's property is bordered by the San Joaquin Nature Preserve (below) and the UCI arboretum. Alexa Bach

site improvement. Construction costs were $58.5 million, while soft costs—including architectural fees, legal expenses, marketing, and other services—added another $45.9 million.

Construction financing was provided by Bank of America and several participating banks. Financing from bank sources totaled $128 million, while financing from mezzanine sources totaled $35.4 million. All financing was provided at competitive interest rates at the time. The loan agreement did not have a presale requirement because Building A was complete and Building B's core and shell were finished. SRG, the managing member, and Equity Residential, the limited partner, provided equity.

Watermarke LLC bought Watermarke from the previous partnership for $150 million. The Bank of America loan was recapitalized to pay off the previous debt on the asset and the resulting profits from sale were rolled into the equity.

Marketing and Management

SRG emphasizes its marketing technique, believing that buyers will pay more when the presentation is perfect. To promote Watermarke, Regis Homes—an operating affiliate of SRG—relied mainly on the project's highly visible, mixed-use location, market timing, signage, standard newspaper and magazine advertisements, and a special campaign at the nearby UCI campus in an attempt to attract college student buyers. A large sign on the corner of Jamboree Road and Campus Drive was used to advertise the project's luxury amenities, unique design, and reasonable prices.

Advertisements in the *Los Angeles Times* and the *Orange County Register* notified potential buyers of the opportunity to purchase homes in the community. Once on site, buyers were attracted to the vacation-style amenities, the convenient location, the recreational and scenic opportunities in the adjacent natural areas, and the careful combination of common and private space.

The sales office opened in 2004 during October, which, according to Regis Homes, is typically the beginning of a cyclical slow period for attracting buyers. Watermarke, however, had the advantage of being the first midpriced, luxury condominium community in the region. Careful price positioning placed Watermarke as the upscale alternative to standard residential developments in the Irvine area. The community was the first urban village designed in the local market that included townhomes with street-side access. The unique combination of unit types was attractive to a wide range of buyers. All conditions dovetailed into positioning the project as a community, not just a group of condominium units.

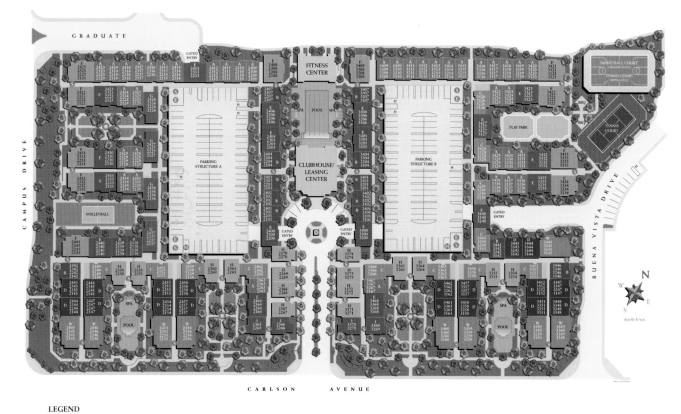

LEGEND

A	B	C	D	E	F	G	H	I	W
Astor Court	Beekman Place	Carlton Arms	Dorchester	Embassy Row	Fifth Avenue	Gramercy Park	Haddon Hall	Imperial House	Waldorf-Astoria

Elevator   Stairs   Mail

Site plan. Sares·Regis Group

The robust sales of Watermarke housing units—all 534 selling within 12 months—suggest that SRG tapped into a market of suburban residents ready for a new, conveniently located community offering a wide range of amenities for an active lifestyle. SRG considered the sales prices reasonable (mid-range) for the area, though no comparable properties existed. One-bedroom units started selling in the low $300,000s, two-bedroom units began in the low $500,000s, and three-bedroom units sold in the $600,000s. SRG saw the quick sell-out as confirmation of its market assumptions.

Most buyers purchased units as is in Building A (phases 7 through 12) because the units were only ten months old. These buyers were offered up to $25,000 off the sales price. About 20 existing renters purchased their units (8 percent retention). Upgrades included choice of different cabinets, countertops, and flooring. The average upgrades were between $20,000 and $50,000. The sales team worked with 30- to 60-day closings. The on-site design center helped secure the quick turnaround.

Several marketing tools helped buyers visualize and customize their units. They included furnished condominium unit models; a three-dimensional community scale model with specific floor plans that lit up on demand; a design center where buyers could select finishes and upgrades; and a display area with giant-size floor plans, aerial photos, and industry recognition awards. Buyers also appreciated the mature vegetation planted around the site and the individual offices for each sales agent.

Watermarke was most popular with first-time buyers—mostly young executives (age 25 to 40), married couples, and singles, living in or moving to the Irvine and South Coast business centers. Empty nesters looking to downsize, second-home buyers, and families with young children have also moved into the community. A handful of parents bought homes for their college-age children.

Watermarke's condominium declaration includes covenants, conditions, and restrictions (CC&Rs) typical for market-rate condominium sales. Originally, the CC&Rs included a pet restriction, required by the city of Irvine because of the community's proximity to the San Joaquin Nature Preserve. City officials were in the process of lifting this restriction in 2006.

In accordance with the declaration, homeowners will pay dues to both a master association (for the Campus Center Master plan of which Watermarke is part) and a subassociation (which solely addresses issues on Watermarke's property) in one monthly bill. Dues to the master association are negligible. SRG budgeted for property management staff members who will take over when the sales team completes closings. Staff members will include three on-site managers, two concierges, and maintenance workers. When Watermarke's homeowners association (HOA) takes over, the salaries and the staff will transition into HOA policy and fees.

Experience Gained

SRG gained valuable experience while introducing Orange County to a new condominium product.

» **Stay on top of the market.** SRG maintained total awareness of the market while it endeavored to present an original product in the highly competitive Irvine area. Detailed architecture, large and detailed floor plans, personalized sales service, and numerous vacation-style community amenities created Irvine's first urban village residential neighborhood and gave Watermarke an advantage over similar-sized communities. In addition, SRG's market consciousness and willingness to change the business plan, as necessary, throughout the development process, permitted greater success and maximized profits.

» **Plan for long-term flexibility.** Upfront condominium mapping and entitlements gave SRG the ability to make flexible and efficient business decisions later.

» **Be creative.** Watermarke was the first community in Orange County to offer residents covered, secured parking on the same level as their home. Other innovative elements, such as resort amenities (including the two-level sports facility), further appealed to buyers.

» **Balance personal and social space.** Buyers were attracted to Watermarke's community events, while at the same time enjoying their privacy. Large, black-iron garage access gates and ample covered parking limit access and provide the ability to park near one's doorstep, while luxury community amenities and events offer social opportunities.

» **Location is still key.** Located in one of Orange County's most desirable cities, Watermarke provides residents the rare opportunity to live adjacent to a natural setting, yet within steps of city conveniences. Location, blended with creative design, maximized the number of units with views of parkland and city lights, thus maximizing revenue.

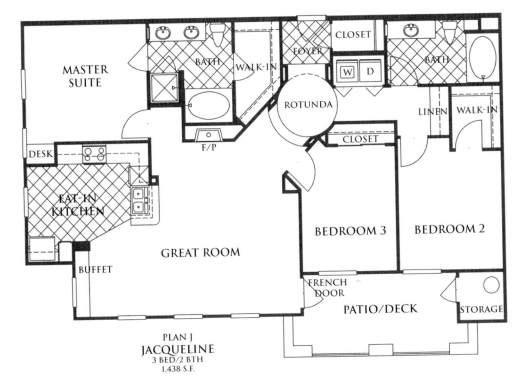

Three-bedroom, two-bathroom floor plan.

Sares·Regis Group

PLAN J
JACQUELINE
3 BED/2 BTH
1,438 S.F.

Project Data: Watermarke

www.watermarkehomes.com

Land Use Information

Site area: 10.81 net acres

Total dwelling units planned: 535

Total condominium units completed: 534 (Two units were merged during the conversion to condominiums)

Average net density: 49.5 units per acre

Land Use Plan

	Acres	Percentage of Site
Attached residential	4.86	45
Roads	1.08	10
Common open space	2.16	20
Parking garage	2.71	25
Total	10.81	100

Residential Unit Information

Unit Type (Bedroom/ Bath)	Number of Units Built	Unit Size (Square Feet)	Range of Sales Prices
1/1	155	635	$311,000–349,000
1/1	60	726	$359,000–416,000
1/1	44	818	$399,000–439,000
1/1 + den	72*	842	$424,000–464,000
2/2	68	1,123	$529,000–589,000
2/2	44	1,250	$549,000–599,000
2/2	16	1,122	$529,000–569,000
2/2.5	32	1,482	$569,000–689,000
2/2.5	8	1,467	$639,000–684,000
3/2	36*	1,438	$629,000–699,000

* A one-bedroom, one-bathroom unit and a three-bedroom, two-bathroom unit were combined at a buyer's request.

Development Cost Information

Site acquisition cost	$ 34,643,000
Site improvement cost	10,688,400
Construction cost	58,495,200
Soft cost	45,885,700
General conditions	3,387,700
Total development cost, excluding cost of capital	**$153,100,000**
Total development cost for apartments	116,200,000
Total development cost for condominium transformation and Building B completion	36,900,000
Cost of capital (equity)	30,000,000
Total development cost	**$ 183,100,000**

Development Schedule

Site purchased:	December 2001
Planning started:	January 2001
Construction started:	January 2002
Sales started:	October 2004
First closing:	December 2004
Phase 1 completed:	December 2004
Sold out:	October 2005
Project completed:	December 2005

Project Team

Developer and Site Planner
Sares·Regis Group
Irvine, California
www.sares-regis.com

Landscape Architect
Lifescapes International
Irvine, California
www.lifescapesintl.com

Architect
Meeks + Partners
Newport Beach, California
www.meekspartners.com

Structural Engineer
Dale Christian Engineering
Orange, California
www.dalechristian.com

Parking Garage Architect
Parkitects
Irvine, California
www.parkitects.com

Soils Engineer
Pacific Soils
Tustin, California
www.pacificsoils.com

Civil Engineer
Keith Companies
Irvine, California
www.keithco.com

ZOCALO

Santa Fe, New Mexico

The concept for Zocalo began with developer Don Tishman's dream of creating an exquisitely designed but affordably priced residential community with high-quality amenities in the dramatic New Mexico landscape. Tishman was particularly inspired by the work of renowned Mexican architect Ricardo Legorreta, whose firm designed the new Visual Arts Center at the College of Santa Fe.

Zocalo is a condominium community located on nearly 47 acres on the outskirts of Santa Fe, New Mexico. At buildout, the project is planned to include a total of 320 units, 11 percent of which are affordably priced. This project was the first time Legorreta applied his skills to a moderately priced residential project.

Background

Don Tishman is a seasoned real estate professional now based in Santa Fe. Throughout his career, he has developed more than 40,000 multifamily dwellings in more than 30 major markets in the United States, in addition to shopping centers, office buildings, and industrial parks. For the Zocalo project he teamed up with Jack Westman, an engineer and general contractor who has been actively involved in engineering, construction, and real estate development in New Mexico for 30 years. Other partners include Edward Gilbert, Snow Moore, and Will Browning. The resulting company, Foothills Estates, LLC, carried out the project.

Legorreta + Legorreta, based in Mexico City, was responsible for the project site plan as well as building design. Ricardo Legorreta is one of the world's most honored architects, and his firm is known for its attention to design detail and the ability to blend strong building forms, light, space, and color. Much of Legorreta's work has focused on public buildings and luxury homes throughout the world; a moderately priced condominium project such as Zocalo was something new for him. Albuquerque architecture firm Dekker/Perich/Sabatini was responsible for melding the design concepts with the practical realities of complying with local regulations and meeting the demands of building contractors.

Creating a cutting-edge design that is compatible with the city's environment and architectural flavor is a challenge for any developer in Santa Fe. The city's history dates back 400 years and it embodies elements of the Native American, Spanish, and American West cultures that have left a mark there. Many buildings in Santa Fe combine elements of historic Spanish and Pueblo Indian adobe architecture. In 1957, the city enacted a historic preservation ordinance, mandating that all new and rebuilt buildings within historic areas be in the Pueblo Re-

vival style of architecture. Over the years, adherence to a relatively strict interpretation of the acceptable design details and colors for new development has helped create a distinctive architectural character in Santa Fe. The city maintains style and color uniformity through a point system in which components of a project can either earn or lose points.

Planning and Construction

The 47-acre project site is located four miles from the center of Santa Fe on the northwest edge of the city, in an area that is still largely undeveloped but now emerging as a growth corridor. Typical of Santa Fe's high desert environment, it features a dry, hilly terrain with scrub and sagebrush vegetation, piñon trees, and dry creeks known as arroyos. Views south from the site look out to Santa Fe and the distant Sandia Mountains.

Several environmental conditions on the site, such as historic streambeds and a rolling topography with steep hillsides, created site-planning challenges. To develop portions of the site near the arroyos it was necessary to rechannel stormwater, create water detention ponds, and pipe excess water into

Zocalo is a mixed-income condominium community located on nearly 47 acres on the outskirts of Santa Fe, New Mexico. Architect Ricardo Legorreta and his Mexico City–based firm, Legorreta + Legorreta, strayed from their typical focus on public buildings and luxury homes to conceive the more moderately priced Zocalo development. Alan Stoker Photography

Attached units are arranged in clusters reminiscent of small-scale village plazas or zocalos. Lourdes Legorreta

Site-planning challenges were presented by historic stream-beds and steep hillsides. In order to develop portions of the site near the arroyos, storm-water was rechanneled, water detention ponds were created, and excess water was piped into the larger streams on or near the site. Lourdes Legorreta

the larger streams on or near the site. Considerable care was taken in regard to the topography. The city allowed building on a maximum area of 106,000 square feet of steep slope areas (areas with 10 to 30 percent slope angles). Much of the existing vegetation was retained in spite of the higher costs involved in construction.

Before the developer of Zocalo bought the site, it was owned by Security Capital, which originally planned to construct 450 smaller, for-rent residential units there. The Zocalo site plan approved by the city allows a maximum of only 323 units because of the increased square footage per condominium. The number of units was reduced to lessen the impact on the site. Plans call for five phases. Phases 1 and 2 with 110 condominium units have been completed. Planning and marketing for Phase 3 began in mid-2005. In an effort to broaden the target market and attract buyers for more moderately priced units, this phase will be made up of 46 lofts, ranging in size from 1,039 to 1,467 square feet. Phase 4 is in the design phase, and plans for Phase 5 were still uncertain as of early 2006.

Phases 1 and 2 feature densities of six to seven units per acre. In future phases, densities are planned to increase to 12 or more units per acre. In spite of higher density, the impact on the site is expected to decrease because of greater consolidation and more stacking of buildings on the site.

The city of Santa Fe closely monitors the development process to ensure that it conforms to the approved plan, so the developer was careful to document site plan changes and ensure that they were allowable. Therefore, amending the Site Development Plan was necessary at both Phase 1 and Phase 2. This process was not onerous, but it did take about three months to complete. When the city took longer than anticipated, the developer was able to obtain permission from city staff to submit plans for building permit plan review concurrently with the site development plan approval, saving future time.

In Phase 1, many of the units were arranged on individual building pads set on stepped terraces following the profile of the hilly terrain. Those individual building pads required the construction of numerous retaining walls to stabilize the land between elevation changes. Although these walls provide an attractive outdoor patio feature for homeowners, they are an expensive solution to terrain management. In subsequent phases, plans exist to grade more extensively and create areas for multiple buildings to be placed on larger building pads.

One issue that arose during development of the first phases was the exterior paint color. Most buildings in Santa Fe adhere to a fairly narrow palette of earth tones, and the more dramatic "gingerbread" color specified by Legorreta was considered unacceptable by neighbors in the area. As a compromise, a more indigenous earth tone was used on the condominium facades facing neighbors to the west. The remaining exterior colors use the Legorreta palette. Walls that are not visible from outside Zocalo are accented by bright colors such as pink, yellow, blue, and purple.

Construction began in 2001. The first group of 12 condominiums took approximately one and a half years to complete, which is probably longer than average for this type of construction. According to the developer and architect, the careful attention to custom details such as windows and interior door frames took longer than it would have for a standard production project. In some cases, the work had to be redone numerous times to ensure that it met with the designer's intention.

Buildings are wood-frame construction with a stucco finish covered with a breathable elastomeric paint. Such "elastic" wall coverings are flexible coatings five times thicker than latex paint that stretch and shrink in response to temperature changes without cracking. The flat roofs are four-ply built-up roofs with built-in slopes. To prevent noise transfer, double gypsum partitions are used between units. Plumbing and air-conditioning elements are isolated from the wood framing to avoid vibration noises.

The process of finding building materials and making sure they met with Legorreta's approval was a challenge for the local architects, who were obliged to source only readily available equipment and fixtures in order to meet the project's budget requirements. For example, the facade design called for a specific type of custom window. After considerable research and several design revisions, the final solution was a premanufactured aluminum-clad wood window. Light fixtures, door details, and casework were similarly translated from Legorreta-inspired designs into standardized products and methods.

Financing

Zocalo was largely financed through the sales of condominium units, although a construction loan was necessary in the early phases to supplement the partners' original equity of $3 million. Initial lender appraisals for the project were low because of the lack of comparable projects in the area. Therefore, it was necessary to sell 20 units before a loan for 80 percent of appraised value was obtained. The loss in income from providing affordable housing at a lower-than-market rate was incorporated into the sales price of the market-rate units.

Affordable Housing Component

Housing affordability is a significant issue in a city where the average wage is 20 percent below the national average and the cost of housing is 53 percent above it, according to the Bureau of Business and Economic Research at the University of New Mexico. In the first quarter of 2005, the median sales price of homes sold through Santa Fe's Multiple Listing Service came in at $365,000, up 16 percent from the same period in 2004.

In the mid-1990s, the city of Santa Fe adopted an inclusionary zoning ordinance known as the Housing Opportunity Program that requires market-rate builders to contribute in some way to providing affordable homes. The city required that 11 percent of the units at Zocalo, or about 40 units, be marketed and sold as affordable housing. In return, the developer received a density bonus and reduced fees for those units. The city defined affordable as within the means of buyers earning 50 to 70 percent of the area median income.

The 30 one-, two-, and three-bedroom affordable units constructed and sold in the first two phases are identical in size and standard finishes to the market-rate condominiums. Construction costs were approximately $170,000. Sales prices for affordable units were based on the buyer's income and ranged from about $98,000 to $145,000. These prices were based on

The city of Santa Fe required the developer to sell 11 percent of Zocalo's condominiums as affordable housing and, in return, provided a density bonus and reduced fees for the affordable units. Lourdes Legorreta

the assumption that 30 percent of a buyer's income would be used for housing and on a calculation of what would be affordable for people earning 50 to 70 percent of the area median income.

The Santa Fe Community Housing Trust (SFCHT) was responsible for establishing a list of income-eligible buyers for Zocalo's affordable units and assisting them in obtaining financing through counseling and homebuyer training programs. The city of Santa Fe holds a second mortgage for each affordable unit that runs parallel with the buyer's 30-year first mortgage. Owners must occupy their units, and resales are severely restricted. The concept is for low-income buyers and the city to share in the appreciation that is expected to occur over time.

Both the developer and SFCHT note that as the first large-scale application of Santa Fe's Housing Opportunity Program, the process worked well.

Design

Zocalo's design takes its cues from the indigenous adobe architecture found throughout the Indian pueblos of northern New Mexico, particularly Taos Pueblo. Features such as flat roofs, stucco surfaces, and simple window openings reinforce this traditional appearance. At the same, Zocalo is strikingly modern. The focus on window placement, lack of exterior adornment, and bold color accents combines with geometric building forms to create a contemporary look.

The attached units are arranged in clusters that follow the rolling site topography and provide an image of small-scale village plazas, or *zocalos*. Each unit has a garage fronting the street, a small entry courtyard, and private patio or deck.

The condominium units in Phases 1 and 2 include a mix of two- and three-bedroom units ranging in size from 1,115 to 2,400 square feet. In Phase 3, the smallest model is 1,039 square feet on one level with one bedroom, one bathroom, and an open living/dining area. It is marketed as a live-in studio space or easily accessible, open-plan condominium home. The two-bedroom units range in size from 1,318 to 1,467 square feet.

Zocalo's interior design features include open living areas with high ceilings, expansive windows, carefully finished wall surfaces, flush wood doors, and a Legorreta-specified color scheme. Standard features include kitchen appliances, ceramic tile kitchen and bathroom countertops and tub surrounds, spacious closets, recessed lighting, and prewiring for cable television and high-speed Internet. Larger units have in-floor radiant heating with a separate evaporative or refrigerated air-cooling system, while smaller units have fan coil heating and cooling. A range of upgrades, such as stainless steel kitchen appliances, designer tiles, and flooring, is available at additional cost. Floor plans are fixed and cannot be modified.

Focus groups, made up mostly of local Realtors, provided valuable input into the design of the units. For example, members of this group suggested that *vigas*, or traditional ceiling beams, were considered highly desirable by potential buyers, so this design feature was incorporated in the units of Phases 1 and 2.

Amenities are an important feature of Zocalo. A 5,700-square-foot clubhouse near the entrance to the development includes a fitness center, swimming pool, club room, confer-

Zocalo's design—with flat roofs, stucco surfaces, and simple windows—is based on the indigenous adobe architecture found throughout northern New Mexico, while the window placement, lack of exterior adornment, and geometric forms create a contemporary look.
Lourdes Legorreta

Site plan. Dekker/Perich/Sabatini

Focus groups suggested that "vigas," or traditional ceiling beams, were considered highly desirable by potential buyers, so they were incorporated in the units of Phases 1 and 2.

Alan Stoker Photography

ence room, and catering kitchen. This $1 million facility also serves as a marketing center and a showpiece for the project's characteristic design.

Although Zocalo was not designed or constructed with particular attention to environmental sustainability, it does feature several energy- and water-saving features. Windows on western exposures have low-E (low-emittance) tinted glass to discourage heat gain. The landscaping throughout the project is all natural xeriscaping that is drought-tolerant and requires little water. In addition, rainwater is collected throughout the site in small cisterns.

Marketing and Sales

The original concept envisioned by the developer anticipated that the primary market for Zocalo would be second-home buyers. The importance of this group was also pointed out in early feasibility studies performed by consultants Robert Charles Lesser & Company.

On the basis of sales in Phases 1 and 2, the market has proven to be a mix of both full- and part-time residents—the breakdown is estimated at 60 percent first-time homebuyers and 40 percent buyers of second homes. Full-time residents include retirees downsizing to smaller homes, working professionals from Santa Fe and nearby Los Alamos, plus a small sprinkling of families with children.

Santa Fe has a strong short-term rental market during the summer months and at Christmas. Zocalo does not have an in-house rental program, but some individual owners rent their units through outside real estate management companies.

The development is marketed through its real estate agents, French & French Sothebys International. A common

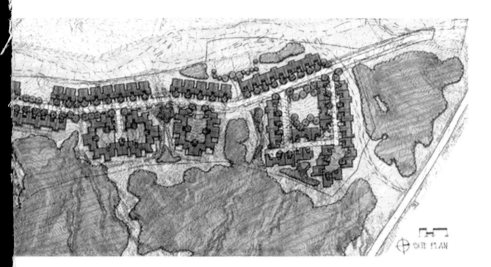

SITE PLAN

theme with buyers is an interest and involvement in the arts and design, and the design by Legorreta + Legorreta has been a unique marketing tool. Zocalo's Web site is also important. It features photos of the project and individual units, as well as floor plans. The project is also advertised in magazines such as *Santa Fe,* which is distributed in hotel rooms as well as through subscriptions. Developer Tishman notes that the goal is not to attract buyers to Santa Fe, but to encourage them to consider Zocalo once they arrive.

As of summer 2005, the first two phases of the project were completed and sold. By this time planning had begun for Phase 3. In spite of a lack of show models or marketing materials, 80 percent of these were sold before groundbreaking.

The average sales price of market-rate units in the early phases was about $250,000. In late 2005, prices ranged from the low $300,000s to over $500,000 for two- and three-bedroom units with up to three bathrooms.

The resale market for Phase 1 and 2 condominiums has been strong. Units that originally sold for $175 per square foot were on the market for $300 per square foot in late 2005.

Experience Gained

The developer considers Zocalo a success. Projections for a 20 percent internal rate of return and sales of 50 units per year were met in the early phases. The attention received by the development will benefit future phases as they come on the market.

» High-quality design can pay large dividends. Marketing experience at Zocalo has proven the significance of the association with an internationally known architect, even for a condominium development at the moderate end of the luxury range. As noted by Tishman, the cost of architectural design is small compared to total project cost, and it can pay big dividends.

» Detailed architecture can lengthen the development schedule. The cost of building beautifully designed projects is not necessarily higher than standard design, but dogged attention to details can add to the length of the construction period and development costs. Achieving the designer's vision on the first phases of the Zocalo project required extra time and effort.

» Multifloor units were less popular with the target market. In the first phases, some of the condominium units featured raised living spaces. Although this design afforded more expansive views for residents, it required walking up one flight of stairs from the entry to the living areas. This configuration proved to be less popular than expected, so plans were modified to create more units with ground-floor living spaces.

» Several changes are planned to reduce construction costs in the future. The amount of site grading and the number of retaining walls will be minimized by reducing the number of individual building pads. There will also be an effort to avoid building in drainage areas.

Project Data: Zocalo

www.zocalosantafe.com

Land Use Information

Site area: 46.45 acres

Total dwelling units planned: 323

Total dwelling units completed: 156
 (market rate and affordable)

Gross density: 6.95 units per acre

Land Use Plan

	Acres	Percentage of Site
Attached residential	13.75	30.0
Roads/drives	5.50	12.0
Common open space	2.20	4.5
Landscaping, patios, trails, drainage areas, undeveloped open space	25.00	53.5
Total	**46.45**	**100.0**

Residential Unit Information (Market Rate)

Unit Type (Bedroom/ Bath)	Number of Units Built	Unit Size (Square Feet)	Range of Sales Prices
Phase 1			
2/2	21	1,115–1,477	$195,000–325,000
2/2.5	42	1,605–1,800	$295,000–344,000
3/2–3.5	16	1,432–2,504	$210,000–525,000
Phase 2			
2/2 or 2.5	18	1,115–1,811	$289,000–405,000
3/2 or 3.5	13	1,432–2,504	$210,000–525,000
Phase 3			
1/1	20	1,039	$295,000–315,000
2/1	20	1,318	$375,000
2/2.5	6	1,467	$422,500

Development Cost Information

Site acquisition cost	$ 2,000,000
Site improvement costs	3,500,000
Construction cost	27,000,000
Soft costs	3,000,000
Total development cost (to date)	**35,500,000**
Total development cost expected at buildout	$ 50,000,000

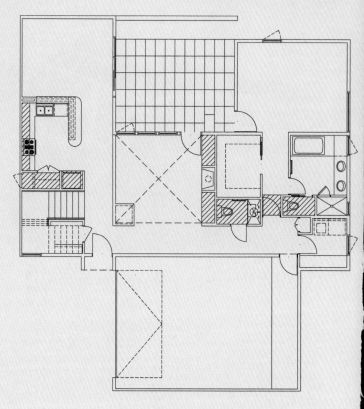

First Floor Unit E

Development Schedule

Site purchased:	July 1999
Planning started:	October 1999
Construction started:	February 2001
Sales started:	Summer 2001
First closing:	Winter 2002
Phase 1 sold out:	Summer 2003
Phase 1 completed:	Fall 2003
Phase 2 sold out:	Summer 2004
Phase 2 completed:	Summer 2005
Project completed:	Projected for fall 2008

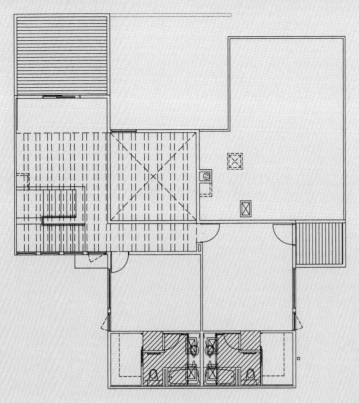

Second Floor Unit E

Three-bedroom, 3.5-bathroom condominium floor plan. Dekker/Perich/Sabatini

Project Team

Developer
Foothills Estates LLC
Partners: Donald Tishman,
   Jack Westman, Edward
   Gilbert, Snow Moore,
   Will Browning

Tishman Group
Santa Fe, New Mexico

Westman Investments
Corrales, New Mexico
www.westmaninvestments.com

Master Planner and Designer
Legorreta + Legorreta
Col. Lomas de Reforma
México D.F. 11020
www.legorretalegorreta.com

Architect
Dekker/Perich/Sabatini
Albuquerque, New Mexico
www.dpsabq.com

Marketing Agents
French & French
Sotheby's International
   Realty
Santa Fe, New Mexico
www.french-french.com

Colophon

This book was composed by Marc Alain Meadows on a Macintosh Power Mac G4 computer running OSX and using QuarkXpress v4.11.

The main text font is the 1989 digitized edition of Syntax, originally designed by the renowned Swiss typographer Hans Edward Meier. Meier created the font for the D. Stempel AG foundry, which released it in 1968 as its last hot-metal type family. Syntax was the first typeface to build upon the modern fonts of Helvetica and Univers by incorporating earlier humanist principles. In 1954, Meier's original drawings for Syntax were derived from brushed letterforms that were traced and redrawn to their essential linear structure, after which the characters were refined and balanced. By combining old-style characteristics that express the rhythm of written letterforms with an optically monoline treatment, Meier created a typeface that is categorized as a legible sans serif. In 2000, Meier reworked the entire Syntax family and it was rereleased by Linotype GmbH as Linotype Syntax™.

Developing Condominiums: Successful Strategies is bound in Toyo Saifu cloth and was printed and bound by Everbest in Hong Kong, China.